The Top
One Hundred
Pasta Sauces

By the same author

Eating out in Italy

The Top One Hundred Italian Dishes

More Great Italian Pasta

Favourite Indian Food

Diane Seed's Mediterranean Dishes

Italian Cooking with Olive Oil

*Diane Seed's Roman Kitchen or
Rome for all Seasons*

The Top 100 Italian Rice Dishes

*Love food, Love Rome or The Food Lover's Guide
to the Secrets of Gourmet Rome*

The Top One Hundred Pasta Sauces

AUTHENTIC RECIPES
FROM ITALY

Diane Seed

■ SQUARE PEG

Published by Square Peg 2012

2 4 6 8 10 9 7 5 3 1

Copyright © Diane Seed 2012

Artwork by Kate Bland

Diane Seed has asserted her right under the Copyright, Designs
and Patents Act 1988 to be identified as the author of this work

First published in Great Britain in 1987 by Rosendale Press

This edition published in 2012 by
Square Peg
Random House, 20 Vauxhall Bridge Road,
London SW1V 2SA

www.vintage-books.co.uk

Addresses for companies within The Random House Group Limited can be found at:
www.randomhouse.co.uk/offices.htm

The Random House Group Limited Reg. No. 954009

A CIP catalogue record for this book
is available from the British Library

ISBN 978 0 22 409532 7

The Random House Group Limited supports The Forest Stewardship Council (FSC),
the leading international forest certification organisation. All our titles that are printed
on Greenpeace approved FSC certified paper carry the FSC logo. Our paper procurement
policy can be found at www.rbooks.co.uk/environment

Printed and bound in Germany by GGP Media GmbH, Poessneck

For Antonio, who first taught me to
appreciate good pasta

Contents

Introduction

Pasta has always been the glory of Italian food, and a symbol of Italian national pride. Today, Italian pasta, like Italian fashion, delights the world.

Nutritionists daily publish new support for 'the Mediterranean diet' as the healthiest and most natural food for us all, low in fat, moderate in protein, high in vitamins and carbohydrates. And that diet is founded on vegetables, fish, and pasta. Pasta itself is not fattening, though some sauces inspire caution. Cooks of many nationalities, whether offering unusual dishes for demanding friends, attempting to fill hungry families, or needing something fast after the office, frequently find they can solve their menu problems by turning to pasta. Pasta dishes are infinitely varied: delicious, usually economical, largely vegetarian, can be fast and simple or complicated and extravagant according to mood.

Perhaps the one strength of which the non-Italian pasta cook is unaware is this variety. Even quite expert cooks often know only half a dozen pasta sauces. Yet the different regions of Italy yield many local specialities and numerous variations on national themes that have been tried and tested over generations. The fresh green vegetable sauces of Puglia in the southern 'heel' of Italy, the rich pork and tomato *ragù* of Naples, the delicate saffron and courgette-flower confection of the Abruzzi region, the aubergine recipes of Sicily, and the lemon sauces of the Amalfi coast all contribute to the amazing versatility of pasta as the foundation of innumerable meals. In the areas around Milan and Venice, traditionally dominated by rice, new pasta sauces are making increasing inroads. Italians eat pasta every day and they are not a people amused by monotony. Pasta has to appear in many guises to continue to arouse applause.

In this book, I have drawn together one hundred of the best pasta sauce recipes, encountered after many years of living, eating and cooking in Italy. Many of them are simple sauces that can be cooked in a few minutes. Others are elaborate confections from the kitchens of great Italian families. All of them adapt well to the needs of other countries, and other climates. However, it would be as well to remember that in Italy pasta is served as an entrée dish before the meat course, while outside Italy it is frequently thought of as the main course itself, and served with simply a salad to follow. In allowing for this, I have recommended quantities for all the pasta variations to feed four to six: an ample dinner for four hungry people, or sufficient for six elegant diners who will then move on to a main course, as in Italy.

How to serve pasta in the Italian style

Although pasta dishes are now eaten with equal enthusiasm from California to Australia, outside Italy they often do not taste as good as they could. But with time, and the knowledge of the following basic rules, we can all learn to perfect our pasta.

Top quality pasta

First and foremost, Italians make sure that the pasta itself takes priority and they know that no sauce, no matter how exquisite, will make the dish come right if the pasta itself is second-rate. This means buying good pasta to start with, from a reliable manufacturer of dried pasta or a high quality specialist shop making its own fresh pasta. If in doubt, I would always choose good quality dried pasta rather than doubtful or even stale 'fresh' pasta. The best durum wheat pasta is pressed through bronze dies. The metal is not completely smooth so the extruded pasta has a rough surface that attracts the sauce. Look for 'bronze die' on the packet. De Cecco, available worldwide, is popular throughtout Italy and use bronze dies. Another good pasta is Voiello but this is no longer exported. Pasta produced with teflon dies is too smooth and in many cases it repels the sauce. The pasta produced in Gragnano, in the province of Naples, is excellent although less widely distributed outside Italy.

A pan for pasta

A very large, tall, good quality pan in which to boil sufficient water for the pasta is also a necessity: every 500g/1lb of pasta needs to be cooked in at least 4 litres/7 pints of water and about 2 tablespoons of salt. Bring the water to the boil and add the salt. With the water boiling briskly add all the pasta at the same time. Long pasta should be eased in and never broken. Stir the pasta every so often with a wooden fork to ensure that it stays separate. Bring the pasta and water back to the boil and boil briskly in an uncovered pan. In Italy we always use coarse sea salt to cook pasta. In my early years in Rome I asked 'why' and the usual answer from everyone, including chefs, was 'because you do'. When I used fine salt on my return visits to London I found it very difficult to get the correct level of salt. Over the years I have come to the conclusion that as coarse salt takes longer to dissolve, the pasta absorbs the salt gradually.

Timing: the essential skill

Italians fuss over perfectly cooked pasta as the French over a soufflé or the English over well-made tea. Pasta should always be firm and provide some resistance or 'bite', as the Italians say, *al dente*. The old Neopolitan description was *vierdi* or 'green' as in slightly unripened fruit. Pasta, after all, is largely a texture.

In Italy no one dreams of adding the pasta to the boiling water until those who are going to eat it are actually present. Restaurants cook pasta freshly for every customer and do not understand impatient tourists who fret about the delay at the start of the meal. Instant pasta invariably means bad pasta, so everyone should be prepared to wait for it to be freshly cooked. The golden rule is 'the sauce waits for the pasta'. The water is ready boiling but the pasta is never thrown in until the sauce is ready. Pasta baked in the oven is the only kind that can be prepared in advance, which makes a dish like Baked Pasta and Artichokes (see page 9) ideal for formal entertaining.

Italian husbands about to leave their office used to say, '*Butta la pasta*' – 'throw in the pasta' – in other words, 'I'm on my way'. Italian traffic has changed all that and woe betide the wife who takes him literally and actuallys starts to cook it before he is safely home. Overcooked pasta is rejected with a curl of the lip and the verdict, '*Scotta*' – overcooked – is a death sentence – to the pasta! Once overcooked it is always thrown away or given to the animals.

Most packets of dried pasta give directions for cooking, usually suggesting 8 to 10 minutes in boiling water. This is a general indication. Most Italians hover over the pan, lifting out a strand from time to time to make sure it is perfect. The ideal way to cook pasta is to make the sauce in a pan large enough to contain the cooked pasta. The drained pasta is then stirred into the sauce for the last few minutes before serving. Keep the pasta water because often a ladleful is stirred into the pan before serving. Egg pasta usually takes less time than flour and water pasta. For fresh pasta, ask the specialist shop what they recommend; 3 minutes or so is usually enough. But no Italian ever trusts such directions completely. An Italian never leaves the kitchen while the pasta is cooking and in the early days I used to scandalise my Roman friends by occasionally walking away from the boiling pot for a second or two.

Unless you are an experienced cook it is best to make the sauce first and leave it to one side to be warmed only, or have a little cream stirred in while the pasta is cooking. You can then give the pasta the benefit of your full attention. Stand over the saucepan, and every so often lift out a strand or piece of pasta to nibble. When it is a little too hard, that is the moment to turn off the heat and drain the pasta. The time that this takes will finish the cooking.

Getting the proportion right

The proportion of sauce to pasta is also a crucial question involving some skill. Italians would criticise foreign cooks intent on producing the authentic dish for a superabundance of sauce. This is one area where 'the more the better' does not apply. The sauce is literally a sauce, intended to coat the pasta strands or shapes and add its flavour to every mouthful. But it should never become a soup, swilling around on the dish after the pasta has been eaten. In the following recipes, I have advised proportions that non-Italians may at first find stingy, and some cooks may prefer to increase the sauce quantities. But if the pasta is really well stirred (and for this a large pan is very important) so that the pasta is very thoroughly coated with the accompanying sauce, this should not really be necessary.

Of course, there is always competition for the sauce. And the last portion in the serving bowl is usually the most delicious. In a typical Roman *trattoria* the woman is served first and then the man is traditionally presented with his portion to eat directly from the serving bowl. When I finally rebelled and demanded my turn to eat from the serving bowl, the waiters received my request with consternation as if the last bastion of male privilege had been threatened.

Cheese: the vital extra

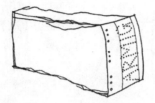

Few cooks outside Italy are aware either of the importance for the final flavour of mixing freshly cooked pasta with freshly grated Parmesan *before* the addition of the sauce. This is not a process that is called for in every recipe, but it makes, for instance, Spaghetti Maria Grazia (see page 48), a dish of pasta and courgette, a memorable treat, while the combination without cheese or with cheese added at table might be much less interesting.

Needless to say, any cheese used with pasta must be freshly grated. Never use packets of ready-grated cheese. Parmesan is expensive, but it is often the only extravagant item in the whole dish. Fresh Parmesan can be bought at most supermarkets and it will keep well wrapped in foil in the refrigerator. The best Parmesan will be marked 'Parmigiano-Reggiano' on the rind. Freshly ground black pepper is also a must in many pasta dishes. Pecorino cheese can be substituted in some of the more robust sauces to get an authentic regional flavour. Cheese is NEVER served with seafood sauces, and pecorino cheese works better with garlic and chilli sauces.

Pasta: different ingredients and different shapes

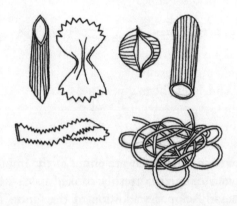

There are two kinds of pasta: that made with durum hard wheat flour and water, and that made with durum or soft flour and eggs. Both kinds of pasta can be dried and are sold in packets. Only soft flour and egg pasta is sold fresh or made at home, with one or two regional exceptions.

Hard Wheat and Water Pasta

Hard wheat and water pasta is used for round pasta strands such as spaghetti and is suited to olive oil-based, robust sauces that make the pasta slippery and flavour it strongly with garlic and tomato. Since the durum wheat for this kind of pasta was grown around Naples, as early as the 16th century, Naples became the centre for the techniques of machine kneading and drying for wholesale consumption. Pasta dough made from durum wheat is too hard and brittle to knead by hand. Drying the hard pasta, always a tricky process since pasta dried too slowly goes mouldy and pasta dried too fast cracks and breaks, originally took place out of doors. The ancient streets and courtyards of old Naples were habitually strung not with washing but with pasta hung out to dry. The area around Torre Annunziata and Torre del Greco, where a combination of hot winds from Vesuvius and cool breezes from the sea were said to change the temperature four times a day, became the centre of the drying and, later, the manufacture of pasta. This tradition is kept alive in Gragnano where some of the most prized pasta is manufactured.

In the Naples area, the appetite for macaroni, as pasta was called, proved enormous from the start. Street vendors fished macaroni from boiling cauldrons, and sold it sprinkled with a little cheese and black pepper for a mere two grani. This pasta was eaten with the fingers, the local populace throwing their heads back and raising their eyes to heaven as they lowered the strands into their mouths. Ingenuous foreign visitors marvelled at the sight and assumed that the poor were thanking God for their daily pasta. Even aristocratic Neapolitans ate spaghetti with their hands and for this reason it was not served at court. Finally, Ferdinand II baulked at this deprivation, and his advisers invented the short four-pronged fork to allow their sovereign to eat his pasta with dignity.

French chefs imported by the richest families – the Neapolitan name for 'chef' was *monzù*, a corruption of *monsieur* – had to learn to embellish pasta, and some of the meat sauces I have included as well as the 'special occasion' dishes show their influence.

Flour and Egg Pasta

Flour and egg pasta was invented in the rich pastures of the central Emilia-Romagna region of Italy. According to tradition, egg pasta made its first appearance in 1487 for the marriage of Lucrezia Borgia to the Duke of Ferrara, when the cook Zafirano wished to compliment her golden curls and rolled the pasta sheets into coils, cutting them into ringlets.

These delicate golden sheets of pasta, with 2 eggs to every 200g/7oz of flour, are used for most stuffed pasta, and cut into ribbons for tagliatelle and the thinner taglionini or tagliarini. Egg pasta is ideally suited to mild cream and butter-based sauces, with additions such as green asparagus, or ham and peas.

Ideas for Leftover Pasta

In Italy even the animals love pasta. Pet food manufacturers produce pasta for dogs, and in Rome every day one sees colonies of stray cats being fed leftover pasta.

Some leftovers are too tasty to be thrown away and they can be used to make delicious snacks or appetisers. I often make an extra quantity of spaghetti with pesto sauce so that I can use it the next day with beaten eggs to make a delicious omelette. Most pasta with a strongly flavoured sauce can also be fried directly in olive oil without eggs to make a crisp, brown round like a thick pancake.

But writing and reading about pasta and its tradition is hungry work. Let's make for the kitchen. *Butta la pasta!*

Please note
All recipes are for 4 people as a main course
or for 6 people as a starter.

The following general US conversions cover the ingredients used in this book.

For milk/stock/wine 250ml = 1 cup

For double (heavy) cream 200ml = 1 cup

For grated Parmesan or similar 100g = 1¼ cups

For grated fontina/Emmenthal or similar 100g = 1 cup

For ricotta or similar curd cheese 100g = ½ cup

For butter 15g = 1 level tbsp/100g = 1 stick

For flour 15g = 1 level tbsp/130g = 1 cup

For small or roughly chopped nuts 100g = ¾ cup

For pine nuts or finely chopped nuts 100g = 1 cup

For dried beans 100g = ½ cup

For shelled fresh peas 100g = ¾ cup

For shelled broad (fava) beans 100g = ⅔ cup

For chopped onion 100g = ⅔ cup

For lentils 100g = ⅔ cup

For black olives 100g pitted = ¾ cup/ 100g whole = 1 cup

VEGETABLE SAUCES

Artichokes
Carciofi

The Arabs brought the globe artichoke to Italy, and its Italian name *carciofi* is a phoneticised version of the Arabic *kharciof*. Artichokes enjoyed great popularity at the Medici court, and during the Renaissance the artichoke was believed to be an aphrodisiac. In modern Italy it is prized for its high iron and iodine content and its beneficial effect on the liver.

The artichoke appears in many different guises in modern Italian gastronomy. Minute whole pickled artichokes – *carciofini* – appear as antipasto or as snack-bar sandwich fillings. In Rome, young tender artichokes, with their chokes removed, are cooked in oil, white wine and mint. Every part of this artichoke can be eaten and it looks spectacular as it is presented standing on its head with its long stalk in the air. In the old ghetto area, near Marcello's theatre, the same young artichokes are cooked *alla giudia* – 'in the Jewish way' – where the whole artichoke is pressed open until it resembles a water lily. Deep-fried, every delicious, crunchy morsel can be eaten. Artichokes are even used to make an aperitivo – 'Cynar'. The manufacturers claim that this drink alleviates the stress of frantic modern life.

However, the real wealth of the artichoke is best seen in pasta recipes. Although it is difficult to find the small tender artichokes outside the climate of Italy or California, it is quite easy to obtain the purple-leaved, spiky variety, which can be used almost as well.

In my Rome market I buy fresh artichokes that have been trimmed and prepared by the vegetable seller, each artichoke rubbed with lemon to stop it going brown. Artichokes turn brown very quickly once they are cut, so always prepare an acid mixture of water and vinegar or lemon juice before beginning an artichoke-based pasta sauce. Artichokes can also stain the hands quite badly so I advise rubber gloves for the cleaning and chopping.

How to prepare artichokes

1) Remove the tough outer leaves and cut off the spiky, pointed top.

2) Remove the stalk and cut lengthways into 8 segments.

3) Cut away the beard-like choke and discard any tough leaves that might spoil the sauce.

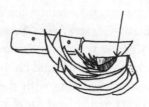

4) Put the artichoke segments into water with vinegar or lemon to prevent discolouration.

Cannelloni ai Carciofi
CANNELLONI WITH ARTICHOKE

18 sheets dried lasagne or dried cannelloni tubes
4 globe artichokes
3½tbsp olive oil
1 onion, finely chopped
2 cloves garlic, finely chopped

250g/9oz minced veal
100ml/3½fl oz dry white wine
1tsp chopped fresh thyme
200ml/⅓ pint chicken stock
1 egg yolk
80g/3oz freshly grated Parmesan
salt and freshly ground black pepper

for the béchamel sauce
80g/3oz butter
80g/3oz flour
600ml/1 pint milk

Preheat the oven to 220°C/425°F/gas 7. Prepare the artichokes.

Heat the oil and gently fry the onion and garlic for 5 minutes. Just before using them, drain and chop the artichokes and add to the onion and garlic along with the veal, stir well and leave to cook over a very gentle heat for 10 minutes. Pour in the white wine and cook for another 10 minutes. Season with the thyme, salt and freshly ground black pepper. Cover and simmer for 15 minutes, adding a little of the chicken stock from time to time to keep the mixture moist.

Meanwhile, make a thick béchamel sauce with the butter, flour and milk. Season well. Mince or process the artichoke mixture at the end of the cooking time, then add the egg yolk, half the freshly grated cheese and about 100ml/3½fl oz of the béchamel sauce. This mixture is used to stuff the cannelloni.

Prepare the pasta, carefully following the packet instructions. If using lasagne sheets, place a little filling on one side of each sheet and then roll up to make a tube. Place the stuffed pasta in a buttered, rectangular oven dish, with the seam at the bottom. If you need to make a second layer, brush the first layer with butter before adding the second. Pour the rest of the béchamel sauce over the filled cannelloni and sprinkle with the rest of the cheese. Bake in the hot oven for about 20 minutes.

Tagliatelle al Carciofi
TAGLIATELLE WITH ARTICHOKES

500g/1lb tagliatelle
4 globe artichokes
2tbsp olive oil
30g/1oz butter
1 small onion, chopped
150ml/¼ pint dry white wine
juice of ½ lemon
150ml/¼ pint chicken or beef stock
200ml/⅓ pint double cream
40g/1½oz freshly grated Parmesan
salt and freshly ground black pepper

Prepare the artichokes (see page 4).

Heat the oil and butter and gently fry the onion until soft. Keep the heat low and cover the pan. Drain and chop the artichokes. After about 5 minutes add them to the pan. Stir, cover again and cook for another 5 minutes. Now add the white wine, lemon juice and stock. Cook gently, covered, for about 20 minutes.

Meanwhile, heat the water for the pasta. Once you have added the pasta to the water, stir the cream into the artichoke mixture and leave uncovered on a very low heat. Season with salt and freshly ground pepper. The sauce will become thick while the pasta is cooking. Be sure not to overcook the tagliatelle.

Drain the pasta and immediately stir in the freshly grated cheese so that all the pasta is coated with the cheese. Now pour on the artichoke sauce and stir vigorously.

Serve at once.

Spaghetti o Penne con i Carciofi
SPAGHETTI OR PENNE WITH ARTICHOKES

500g/1lb spaghetti or penne
4 large globe artichokes
3½tbsp olive oil
2 cloves garlic, chopped
2tbsp chopped parsley
salt and black pepper
Parmesan, to serve

Prepare the artichokes.

Heat the oil and add the chopped garlic. Drain and chop the artichokes and add them to the garlic, covering the pan so that they stew rather than fry. When they are nearly cooked (usually about 20 minutes, but less if the artichokes are really young and tender), add the parsley and salt and pepper to taste. Keep warm.

Cook the pasta, following the packet directions carefully to avoid overcooking. Drain the pasta, reserving about 4 tablespoons of the pasta water. Turn the pasta into a large serving bowl and quickly stir in the artichokes and the reserved pasta water. Serve immediately. A bowl of freshly grated Parmesan should be served separately for those who like to add cheese.

Pasticcio di Carciofi
BAKED PASTA AND ARTICHOKES

9 sheets dried lasagne
6 globe artichokes
2tbsp olive oil
80g/3oz butter
1 onion, finely chopped
a small glass of dry white wine
1tsp thyme, chopped
100g/4oz freshly grated Parmesan
salt

for the béchamel sauce
80g/3oz butter
80g/3oz flour
700ml/1¼ pints milk
½tsp ground nutmeg
salt and black pepper

Preheat the oven to 220°C/425°F/gas 7. Prepare the artichokes.

Heat the oil and butter and add the finely chopped onion. Cover and cook for about 5 minutes. Drain the artichokes well, place the segments in the pan and stir for about 5 minutes. Pour in the wine and season with salt to taste and the thyme. Cover and cook gently for about 20 minutes.

While the artichokes are cooking, heat a large saucepan of water. Salt well and cook the lasagne, one or two sheets at a time, in the boiling water for about 5 minutes. Remove with a slotted spoon and plunge instantly into a bowl of cold water, then lay out on a clean teatowel. Although this process is time-consuming it is necessary to prevent the sheets of pasta sticking together.

Make a béchamel sauce with the butter, flour, milk and seasonings.

Butter a rectangular oven dish and pour in one quarter of the béchamel sauce. Cover this with 3 sheets of lasagne, overlapping them a little. Pour in one third of the remaining béchamel to cover the pasta, and sprinkle one third of the freshly grated cheese over this. Now add half the artichoke mixture, spreading it evenly over all the surface. Cover this with another 3 sheets of lasagne. Pour on half the remaining béchamel sauce and again sprinkle with cheese, using half the remainder. Spread the last of the artichoke mixture evenly over this. Cover with the 3 remaining sheets of lasagne and the rest of the sauce and cheese.

Dot with the remaining butter and bake in the hot oven for about 30 minutes. Remove from the oven and let the dish 'settle' for about 3 minutes before serving.

Asparagus
Asparagi

Green asparagus makes a deliciously different sauce to go with fresh pasta or dried pasta made with egg. Now that the short spring season is extended with imports, asparagus recipes are worth collecting.

Pasta al Forno con Asparagi
BAKED PASTA WITH ASPARAGUS

400g/14oz penne or other short pasta
120g/4½oz butter
1kg/2lb asparagus, washed, tough stalks removed
and cut into short lengths
a little chicken stock
300g/10oz ricotta or similar curd cheese
1tbsp olive oil
120g/4½oz freshly grated Parmesan
3 eggs
salt and freshly ground black pepper

Preheat the oven to 180°C/350°F/gas 4.

Melt 40g/1½oz of the butter in a pan and cook the asparagus over a low heat for about 20 minutes. Every so often, add a little stock to keep moist. When the asparagus is cooked, season to taste.

While the asparagus is cooking, process the ricotta cheese with the oil. Cook the pasta for half the time stated on the packet. Drain and immediately toss in the remaining butter and half the cheese.

Butter a deep oven dish. Make a thin layer of pasta, then one of asparagus, then one of pasta again and then one of ricotta. Repeat, finishing with a layer of pasta.

Beat together the eggs and the remaining cheese and pour over the top. Sprinkle with black pepper. Bake for 20 minutes.

Tagliatelle agli Asparagi
TAGLIATELLE WITH ASPARAGUS

This is a simple recipe but its subtle, delicate taste can remain in the memory for a long time.

500g/1lb tagliatelle, or green and white paglia e fieno
500g/1lb asparagus, washed and tough stalks removed
100g/4oz butter
1 slice stale white breadcrumbs
200ml/⅓ pint double cream
a little chicken stock
50g/2oz freshly grated fontina, Gruyère
or Emmenthal
salt and black pepper

Place the asparagus in a large, shallow pan with a lid, add salt and cover with boiling water. Cook for about 8 minutes if the asparagus is thick, less if thin. Drain and plunge into cold water. Drain again and cut into 2cm/¾ inch lengths.

Melt the butter in a large pan, add the breadcrumbs and cook gently, stirring all the time, for about 2 minutes. Now add the cream and a little stock. Stir well and add the asparagus and black pepper to taste. Cook for about 5 minutes. Keep warm.

Cook the pasta, drain and add to the asparagus sauce. Add the cheese and stir until it has melted. Turn into a hot dish and serve at once.

Aubergines
Melanzane

The Arabs first introduced aubergines – or *melanzane* to give them their Italian name – to Italy, and so it is in Sicily, where the Arab influence was strongest, that we find the treasure-house of aubergine recipes.

The traditional Sicilian aubergine pasta was re-christened 'Spaghetti alla Norma' in homage to the composer, Bellini, who was born in Catania. His great success with his opera, 'Norma', caused his proud fellow citizens to coin a new superlative, *'una vera Norma'* to describe and praise any form of excellence. This became so much a part of the local language that many years later the writer Nino Martoglio, tasting this succulent combination of aubergine and tomato for the first time, signalled his enthusiasm by calling it 'Spaghetti alla Norma'. This new name, at first used only locally, has now become widespread throughout Italy.

Years ago while shopping in Rome's Testaccio market I was surprised to learn that the vegetable fennel has gender. The male fennel is round and fertile-looking while the so-called female fennel is longer and thinner. Having swallowed this, I learned recently that according to some experts aubergines, too, can be male or female, the male of course being the more desirable as it contains fewer seeds.

My neighbour, Angelina, who boasts of being fifth generation *contadina*, or agricultural worker, dismissed this theory rather scornfully as 'newfangled nonsense', so I propose to follow her expert opinion and advise choosing aubergines for their freshness, not their sex. The aubergines should be shiny, with a stretched look. Do not buy them if they are dull or wrinkled. The shape and colour depends on the variety of aubergine, and round or long they taste the same. A few years ago I found small, pearly white aubergines and for the first time understood how they got the name 'eggplant'.

Spaghetti alla Norma
SPAGHETTI ALLA NORMA

500g/1lb spaghetti
5 medium-size or 3 large aubergines
1 x quantity of tomato sauce (see page 90)
200g/7oz freshly grated cheese (dry ricotta salata,
Parmesan or pecorino)
salt
olive oil, for frying

First you need to purge the aubergines of their bitter juices. Remove the stalks and thinly slice one of the aubergines. Place in a colander, sprinkle with salt, then arrange the slices in layers on a chopping board, sprinkling each layer with salt. Put the chopping board on the draining board at an angle, wedging it so that it slopes slightly towards the sink. Then cover with another board and a heavy weight (for example a large saucepan filled with water). Leave to drain for about 45 minutes.

At the end of this period rinse the aubergines, pat them dry and fry in olive oil. Use plenty of oil and fry only a few slices at a time. Do not let them become too crisp. Drain each batch on kitchen paper and keep warm. Dice the remaining aubergines.

Warm your tomato sauce. Cook the pasta and drain while it is still very al dente. Stir in first the grated cheese, then the tomato sauce and diced aubergines. Arrange the aubergine slices over the top and serve at once.

Spaghetti con Melanzane e Noci
SPAGHETTI WITH CREAMED AUBERGINES
AND WALNUTS

500g/1lb spaghetti
3 large or 5 medium-size aubergines
½ x quantity of tomato sauce (see page 90)
3 eggs
15 walnut kernels, ground
a few drops of olive oil
salt and black pepper

Wash the aubergines, dry and prick two or three times before placing them whole in an oven dish. Roast in a hot oven for about 35 minutes until wrinkled and soft. Meanwhile, prepare the tomato sauce and hard-boil the eggs until the yolks are just firm and creamy but not too floury. Shell the eggs and separate the yolks from the whites. The whites can be discarded.

Halve the roasted aubergines and scrape the soft pulp into the ground walnuts. Mix well and add the egg yolks. Mix well again, then add the tomato sauce, salt and pepper to taste and a few drops of olive oil. Turn into a large pan and heat for a few minutes, stirring all the time.

Cook the pasta, drain while still al dente and stir into the pan. Mix well and serve immediately.

Pasticcio di Maccheroni con le Melanzane
BAKED PASTA WITH AUBERGINES

At the corner of Via del Corso and Piazza Venezia, next to Palazzo Doria, is the house where Madame Letizia Bonaparte used to live. There is a strange shuttered balcony where she liked to sit unobserved watching the ever-changing spectacle of street life. Today I have a similar vantage point from my desk, and my working day is enlivened by chanting protest marches, squealing brakes followed by the inevitable crash of metal, police, ambulance and fire engine sirens, and the raised voices of the mad, the bad and the happy. In Madame Bonaparte's day the scene was more colourful but just as noisy, with horse races down the Via del Corso, bands and flamboyant processions for saints' days and Carnival, and elegant carriages sweeping round the square to see and be seen.

Madame Bonaparte is said to have had a healthy appetite and enjoyed the complicated pasta *timballo*, prepared for the Roman Carnival. Luigi Carnacina gives the original recipe, but the combination of sweet pastry casing, lard, giblets, pork, beef and mushrooms makes it too heavy and time-consuming for modern tastes. This simpler *timballo* belongs to the same tradition but it is easier on the arteries!

500g zite or rigatoni
4 aubergines, sliced
1 x quantity fresh tomato sauce (see page 90)
6 basil leaves, torn into small pieces
300g/10oz mozzarella

50g/2oz freshly grated Parmesan
2tbsp stale breadcrumbs
course salt, for purging
olive oil, for frying

Cover the aubergine slices with coarse salt and leave for 30 minutes. Rinse well, dry and fry in batches.

Preheat the oven to 150°C/300°F/gas 2. Cook the pasta until it is pliable but not cooked. Drain and toss in the tomato sauce and basil. Grease a deep ovenproof serving dish and put in a thin layer of pasta. Cover this with a layer of aubergine and a few slices of mozzarella. Sprinkle over some Parmesan and make another layer of pasta. Continue in this way until you have used up all the ingredients, finishing with a layer of aubergine, dotted with small pieces of mozzarella and the breadcrumbs mixed with the remaining Parmesan. Bake for 25 minutes.

Basil

Basilico

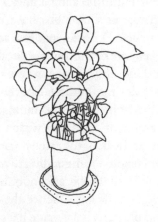

Basil is the most important herb in Italian cooking. Its perfume enhances many dishes, and one of the best ways of serving pasta stuffed with spinach and ricotta is with a simple dressing of melted butter, Parmesan and a few basil leaves. A salad of tomato and mozzarella cheese becomes food for the gods rather than slimmers when three or four basil leaves are tucked between the slices. In general, anything tomato-based benefits from the addition of a few leaves of basil.

Dried basil is not really an acceptable substitute, but before winter frosts kill off the plants it is possible to freeze some leaves to be used later in sauce-making. The flavour is best maintained by packing four or five leaves in a small plastic pot, such as an empty yogurt container. The leaves can then be covered with water and frozen. The frozen block can later be thawed out or added whole to a tomato sauce.

In Genoa, the birthplace of basil, and all along the Ligurian coast, the air is redolent of basil as every available space is filled with every available container, from old saucepans to beautifully painted ceramic pots. The Genovese believe that basil needs a gentle breeze from the sea to bring out its true flavour. Genoa was an independent maritime state, and the sea and the great seafarers like Christopher Colombus have influenced its culinary traditions. The most famous Genovese sauce, pesto, is made of basil that has been worked to form a durable, portable sauce, perfectly suited to long, hazardous voyages of discovery. It has been suggested that during the crusades, the Genovese contingent could be easily identified even as far afield as Jerusalem, by the characteristic aroma of pesto that surrounded them.

Although pesto can be bought ready-made, its glory is appreciated when made at home. Originally, it was a slow, laborious procedure since the basil, garlic and nuts had to be pounded by hand in a pestle and mortar – hence the name 'pesto'. Now food processors and blenders have made it a simple task. Homemade pesto can be frozen very successfully during the summer months.

Pesto requires quite a large quantity of basil and this can provide difficulties in colder countries, but it is possible to grow your own, especially in a greenhouse, conservatory or on a sunny windowsill.

Trenette al Pesto
TRENETTE WITH BASIL SAUCE

500g/1lb trenette, linguine or spaghetti
3 cloves garlic

150g/5oz pine nuts or walnuts or blanched almonds
100g/4oz roughly chopped mixed pecorino,
romano and Parmesan
36 basil leaves (a minimum of 6 per person), sponged and
dried
200ml/⅓ pint good quality olive oil
salt and black pepper
3 small potatoes (optional)
175g/6oz green beans (optional)

Put the garlic, pine nuts and cheese in a food processor and process. While the pasta is cooking, add the basil leaves and the seasoning to the processor. Just before draining the pasta, add the oil to the food processor and process to make a sauce that still has some texture from the Parmesan.

It is usual to garnish the finished dish with slices of boiled potatoes and green beans around the edge of the serving plate. The potatoes are usually cooked with the pasta but it might be easier to boil 2 or 3 potatoes and the beans separately to get the timing right. This garnish is not essential but the potato does seem to make the flavour of the dish smoother.

The pesto sauce is never cooked but 2 or 3 tablespoons of pasta water should be added before the sauce is stirred thoroughly into the drained pasta. Make sure that every strand of pasta is coated with the sauce.

If you are using a large serving plate, arrange the slices of potato and the green beans around the edge, with the pasta in the centre, and with a wooden spoon spread a little pesto over the vegetables. Serve at once. Should there be any left over, a little spaghetti with pesto makes a delicious filling for the next day's omelette.

Black Olives

Olive Nere

The tradition of using olives to make sauces is thought to go back to ancient Roman times. No one knows whether it was the oil or the whole fruit that was first used to flavour food. This Ligurian sauce relies on olives, olive oil and garlic to produce a tasty pasta dish.

Linguine alle Olive
LINGUINE WITH BLACK OLIVES

500g/1lb linguine or spaghetti
2 cloves garlic, chopped
200g/7oz pitted black olives, chopped

3½tbsp olive oil
1tbsp chopped parsley
salt

Soak the garlic and olives in half of the olive oil for several hours, overnight if possible. The olives give out more liquid this way.

While the pasta is cooking, heat the rest of the oil and pour in the olive and oil mixture. Add the chopped parsley and salt to taste. Leave to simmer gently.

Drain the pasta and stir in the olive sauce. Cheese is not usually served with this recipe.

Spaghetti alla Puttanesca
WHORE'S SPAGHETTI

My introduction to this famous pasta dish occurred when I overheard two elderly priests discussing the pros and cons of Spaghetti alla Puttanesca – *Whore's spaghetti* – as they deliberated over the menu in a Neapolitan restaurant. Made of ingredients found in most Italian larders, this is also known as 'Spaghetti alla Buona Donna' – or Good Woman's Spaghetti – which can be misleading if one is not familiar with the ironic insult '*figlio d'una buona donna*'– son of a good woman.

To understand how this sauce came to get its name we have to look back to the 1950s, when brothels in Italy were state-owned. They were known as *case chiuse* or 'closed houses' because the shutters had to be kept permanently closed to avoid offending the sensibilities of neighbours or innocent passers-by. Conscientious Italian housewives always shopped at the local market daily to buy really fresh food, but the 'civil servants' were only allowed one day per week for shopping and their time was valuable. Their speciality became a sauce made quickly from odds and ends in the larder and now invaluable to all of us, whatever degree of virtue, when time and ingredients are in short supply.

500g/1lb spaghetti or vermicelli
1½tbsp olive oil
3 cloves garlic, finely chopped
3 anchovy fillets, chopped
400g/14oz tin Italian plum tomatoes, chopped
120g/4½oz pitted black olives
4tbsp capers
parsley, to garnish

Cook the pasta in a large saucepan. While the water for the pasta is heating put the olive oil in a frying pan. Add the garlic and anchovy and cook gently until they are almost melted. Now stir in the chopped tomatoes with their juice, the black olives and capers. (These can be chopped or left whole according to taste but if the olives are large it is better to chop them.) Cook for 5 minutes.

When the pasta is ready, drain it and add the sauce. Mix well, sprinkle with chopped parsley and serve immediately.

Broad Beans and Peas
Fave e piselli

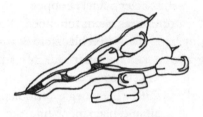

On 1 May it is a Roman custom to eat new, young broad beans raw with salami and pecorino or Parmesan as an appetiser. This combination works well, and is usually accompanied by a glass of robust wine. The beans are heaped on the table still in their pods and everyone shells their own as they go along. Eaten this way they are a special treat and no Festa del Lavoro would be complete without a bean feast! In the past the broad beans were sold by the roadside, and on Sundays in spring many husbands on their way to buy the ritual *dolce* (dessert) for Sunday lunch stopped by the glistening green mounds heaped on the ground to buy an extra *antipasto*. Today this custom has disappeared and, in the market, the stalls selling them have to display a warning because some people who lack a particular enzyme develop a condition known as favism, which can prove fatal. Broad beans are not usually cooked on their own as a vegetable in Italy, but they do appear in vegetable combinations and in pasta sauces.

Pasta con le Fave al Proscuitto
PENNE WITH BROAD BEANS AND HAM

500g/1lb penne or farfalle
1½tbsp olive oil
1 onion, finely chopped
1 stick celery, finely chopped
3 or 4 slices bacon, chopped
400g/14oz shelled broad (fava) beans
100g/4oz cooked ham, cut into thin strips
1tsp sugar (optional)
½ glass white wine vinegar (optional)
salt and black pepper

Heat the oil and add the onion, celery and bacon. Leave to cook gently. Meanwhile, cook the beans in boiling, salted water for about 10 minutes. Drain and add to the bacon mixture. Cook the pasta.

Add the ham to the bean mixture and stir well. Season to taste. If you like a sweet-sour effect, stir in the sugar and wine vinegar. Heat through gently.

Drain the pasta and add to the bean mixture. Turn into a heated dish, stir well and serve. Cheese is not served with this recipe.

Fettuccine con Fave e Pecorino
FETUCCINE WITH BROAD BEANS
AND PECORINO

400g/14oz fettuccine
4tbsp extra virgin olive oil
1 small onion, finely sliced
300g/10oz shelled broad (fava) beans
50g/2oz grated pecorino
1tbsp chopped fresh mint
100g/4oz fresh ricotta
salt and black pepper

Heat the oil in a large pan, add the sliced onion and let it soften without changing colour. Add the beans and stir around for a few minutes before adding 200ml/⅓ pint lightly salted water. Cook for a few minutes until tender. Stir in half the pecorino and a little black pepper. Cook the pasta, drain and stir into the beans. Add the remaining pecorino and mint. Quickly stir in the ricotta mixed with a little pasta water and serve at once.

Tagliolini e Piselli
PASTA WITH FRESH PEAS

In spring, when the small tender peas first appear, they are so good people want to eat them as often as possible, in as many guises as possible, as long as their delicate flavour is not masked. In Testaccio the older stall holders sit shelling the peas with still nimble fingers, while their children get on with the job of selling. If you are in a hurry you can buy small bags of ready-shelled peas, but usually it is a greater pleasure to buy them in pod, so that you can steal the odd pea as you sit at home companionably shelling them.

300g/10oz 1cm/½ inch squares of egg pasta, fresh or dry
2tbsp olive oil
1 onion, chopped
½ stick celery, finely chopped
1 clove garlic, finely chopped
2 rashers streaky bacon, finely chopped (optional)
300g/10oz shelled peas
1tbsp chopped fresh parsley
1.5 litres/2½ pints boiling light stock
6tbsp freshly grated Parmesan, to serve
salt and black pepper

Heat the oil and gently cook the onion, celery, garlic and bacon (if using) until soft. Add the peas, parsley and seasoning and cook gently for 10 minutes. Pour in the boiling stock and, after a few minutes, the pasta.

When the pasta is cooked, serve at once with a generous sprinkling of Parmesan over each serving.

Pasta e Piselli con la Pancetta
PASTA WITH PEAS AND BACON

1½tbsp olive oil
30g/1oz butter
300g/10oz onion, chopped
150g/5oz bacon, cubed
600g/1¼lb fresh or frozen peas, shelled

500g/1lb penne or farfalle
100g/4oz freshly grated Parmesan
salt and black pepper

Heat the oil and butter in a large pan and add the chopped
onion. Cook for about 5 minutes, then add the bacon.

When the bacon is nearly cooked, add the peas. Season to
taste and leave to cook gently.

Cook the pasta for 5 minutes less than the time stated in the
packet directions. Drain and add to the pea mixture, together
with 4 tablespoons of the pasta water. Cover and cook for
another 5 minutes. Do not drain. Serve the freshly grated cheese
separately.

Tagliolini alla Menta
PASTA WITH PEAS AND MINT

This delicate pasta is very simple to make and works very well
even with frozen peas. However you must use fresh mint.

500g/1lb egg pasta like tagliolini or fettuccini
75g/3oz butter
1 small onion, finely chopped

300g/10oz shelled peas
10 mint leaves
50g/2oz freshly grated Parmesan
salt and black pepper

Melt the butter and add the finely chopped onion. When the onion begins to become transparent, add the peas and season to taste. Cover and cook for about 12 minutes. Roughly chop the mint leaves, leaving a sprig for decoration.

Cook the pasta, taking care not to overcook. Drain, stir in the peas, cheese and chopped mint.

Broccoli, Turnip Tops, Greens
Broccoli, Cime di Rape, Broccoletti

Puglia is one of the most interesting and least-known regions of Italy. Its remote position in the 'heel' helped it preserve its secrets, and the gaunt, ruined Saracen towers guarding the coastline remind us that this region was more vulnerable to approaches from the sea than from the land. The land, in fact, is very fertile: some of the best Italian wine and olive oil is produced in Puglia, and the region is famous for the excellence and variety of its green vegetables.

The most characteristic sauce of the region is made from green vegetables and a pasta unique to Puglia – *orecchiette* or 'little ears'. Originally the ears were always brown, made from wholewheat flour, but nowadays a white version is also made from more refined flour. The ears are made by hand and it is fascinating to see the speed with which the local women sculpt these ears from the fresh sheets of pasta.

Some fresh pasta shops outside Italy will make *orecchiette* to order, and it is possible to buy packets of dried *orecchiette*. If you do not find the right pasta shape you can use conchiglie, penne or rigatoni instead. It will not look as interesting but it will taste just as good. I have even used spaghetti at times and I must confess I like the way the greenery twists round the strings of spaghetti.

The traditional green vegetable to use with the following recipe is turnip tops. In Puglia the crop is sown for the tops, not the turnips. I have seen Pugliesi who have 'emigrated' to Rome or Milan returning North with carrier bags sprouting greenery. It is certainly true that the southern *cime di rape* have a distinctive, pungent flavour that is not found in the Rome vegetable. However, this recipe can be made very successfully using purple-flowering broccoli, calabrese or indeed any tender young leafy green vegetable.

Orecchiette con Cime di Rape
ORECCHIETTE WITH TURNIP TOPS

500g/1lb orecchiette or other short pasta
600g/1¼lb turnip tops, broccoli or tender spring (or other)
greens, washed
4tbsp olive oil
5 cloves garlic, chopped
1 or 2 small chilli peppers or 2 tsp dried chilli flakes
salt

Cut the greens into long thin strips. If using broccoli, divide up the florets and slice the stalks in half so that they cook more quickly. Discard the very thick pieces of stalk.

Heat a large pan of salted water and, when it is boiling, plunge in the green vegetables. Do not overcook. They must remain crisp and a good, vivid green. Drain but keep the water.

Bring the water back to the boil and cook the pasta – check that there is sufficient water, adding more if necessary. While it is cooking, heat the olive oil in a large pan. Add the chopped garlic and chilli pepper. (Add the chilli pepper whole for a less hot sauce.) Stir until the garlic is golden brown. Do not allow it to get too dark.

When the pasta is almost ready, put the greens back into the pan with the pasta and cook together for another 3 minutes. Drain carefully, shaking the sieve or colander to remove any water trapped in the crevices of the pasta ears. Turn into a large, warmed serving dish, stir well and add the very hot oil mixture. If the chilli pepper is whole, remove it. Stir well and serve at once. Cheese is not served with this recipe.

Note: Another version of this dish, also from Puglia, adds 6 anchovy fillets, rinsed and finely chopped, to the garlic and chilli during the initial frying period.

Orecchiette con Broccoli e Pomodoro
ORECCHIETTE WITH BROCCOLI AND TOMATOES

500g/1lb orecchiette
600g/1¼lb broccoli
1 x quantity of tomato sauce (see page 90)
80g/3oz freshly grated Parmesan
chopped fresh parsley, to garnish
salt

Cook the broccoli and pasta as in the previous recipe. Add the broccoli to the pasta for the last 3 minutes of cooking. Drain well and put in a hot serving dish. Stir well and add the hot tomato sauce. Stir again, then add the freshly grated cheese. Mix well together, sprinkle with chopped parsley and serve at once.

Cauliflower
Cavolfiore

In Italian markets it is possible to find both the round white cauliflower and the pointed green-flowered variety. They can both be used to make interesting sauces for pasta. The recipes given for broccoli and turnip tops (see pages 32 and 33) can be made very successfully with cauliflower. Here are two additional recipes, including a Sicilian version using nuts and raisins. Nuts and raisins are added to many vegetable sauces in Sicily, due to centuries of Arab influence.

Pasta 'chi Vrocculi Arriminati'
RIGATONI WITH SICILIAN CAULIFLOWER SAUCE

500g/1lb rigatoni
1 cauliflower
2tbsp olive oil
1 onion, finely chopped
1tsp saffron filaments or ¼tsp saffron powder,
dissolved in a little warm water
3 anchovy fillets, chopped
50g/2oz seedless raisins
50g/2oz pine nuts or chopped blanched almonds

50g/2oz freshly grated pecorino or Parmesan
4 chopped basil leaves (optional)
salt

Wash the cauliflower, remove the coarse leaves and cook whole
in boiling, salted water. Do not overcook. While it is still firm,
remove from the water with a slotted spoon; reserve the water.
In a large pan, heat half the oil and add the finely chopped
onion. When it begins to turn colour, add the saffron. Cover
and cook for 10 minutes.

Divide the cauliflower into florets and add to the onion. Heat
the rest of the oil in a small pan and cook the anchovies until
they have almost melted. Add to the cauliflower together with
the raisins and nuts. Stir well and leave, covered, off the heat.
Add more boiling water and salt to the cauliflower water so that
you have enough water to cook the pasta. Follow the packet
directions carefully to avoid overcooking. Drain the pasta and
stir in the cauliflower sauce. Add the freshly grated cheese and
basil, if using. Mix well and serve.

Penne al Cavolfiore
PENNE WITH CAULIFLOWER

500g/1lb penne or other short pasta
1½tbsp olive oil
2 cloves garlic, chopped
1 small chilli
1 cauliflower, divided into florets
230g/8oz tin Italian plum tomatoes, chopped
250ml/8fl oz chicken stock
200ml/⅓ pint double cream

Heat the oil and add the chopped garlic and the whole or chopped chilli pepper. Cook for 10 minutes, then add the cauliflower. After another 5 minutes' cooking, add the chopped tomatoes with their juice. Cook gently for 10 minutes, then add the stock. Leave to simmer while you cook the pasta.

Add the cream to the cauliflower mixture and remove the chilli, if whole. Squash the mixture with a potato masher. Drain the pasta and stir in the sauce at once.

Chickpeas
Ceci

One of the earliest recorded pasta sauces, and certainly one that has a most interesting combination of textures uses plump, firm chickpeas combined with soft boiled pasta and crisp, crunchy pasta that has been fried in olive oil. This contrasting soft and crisp dish is a speciality of Lecce and the Salento Peninsula in the region of Puglia in the southern heel of Italy; it is virtually unknown elsewhere.

The unusual method of frying the dry pasta does not appear in any other existing recipe, but at one time it seems to have been common practice. In the 15th century, a prelate in Florence criticised his congregation's over-elaborate cuisine by upbraiding them: 'It is not enough for you to eat your pasta fried, you think you must add garlic too!'

The frying technique is believed to have developed from the earlier method of rolling out the flour and water paste, baking it on a large, flat stone and cutting the resulting crisp disc into long strips to be added to the other ingredients. The ancient Romans discovered the chickpea recipe when they travelled south to Brindisi on their way to Greece, and the Roman poet Horace, in one of his Satires, writes of the delightful prospect of a plate of pasta and chickpeas awaiting him at home: '*Inde domum me – ad porri et ciceris refero laganique catinum*' ('And so I come home in the evening to eat a bowl of leeks, chickpeas and lasagne').

The dish continued to be enjoyed during the following centuries and became adapted to the dry pasta introduced by the Arabs. It lost its Latin name '*laganelle*' and became '*tria*' from the Arabic '*itrya*', meaning dry pasta with a hole. Today this dish is still called '*ciceri e tria*' – chickpeas and pasta.

After all these hundreds of years the recipe is still a winner. The subtle combination of flavours and textures makes it an interesting, unusual dish. And because of the high-fibre and protein contents of both the chickpeas and pasta the dish appeals to all health-conscious cooks. It is also very economical, and if the dried chickpeas are replaced by tinned chickpeas, a substantial meal can be produced from the store cupboard in 20 minutes.

Ideally, this recipe is best made with dried ribbon-type pasta that does not contain eggs. However, if this is unobtainable it can be made very successfully with dried tagliatelle containing eggs. Green and white pasta could also be used, and adds to the colourful appearance of the final dish. Fresh pasta is not suitable for this recipe. Use good quality olive oil to fry the pasta as this contributes to the final flavour.

Ciceri e Tria
CHICKPEAS AND PASTA

300g/10oz tagliatelle
300g/10oz dried chickpeas or 2 x 425g/15oz tins chickpeas
1tsp bicarbonate of soda (if using dried chickpeas)
1 bay leaf
1 clove garlic
1 onion
1 carrot
1 stick celery
1tbsp chopped fresh parsley
230g/8oz tin Italian plum tomatoes, chopped
salt and freshly ground black pepper
olive oil, to serve

Wash the dried chickpeas (if using) very thoroughly and put them in a bowl with plenty of tepid water. Add the bicarbonate of soda and 1tsp salt to the water. Soak for at least 12 hours.

Drain the chickpeas and put them to boil in plenty of fresh water, with the bay leaf, for 1 hour.

Meanwhile, finely chop the garlic, onion, carrot, celery and parsley together. A food processor is ideal for this.

When the chickpeas have cooked for 1 hour, drain them and return to the pan. Add the chopped vegetables and tomatoes with their juice. Cover with boiling water and cook for another hour, being very careful not to let the pan boil dry.

If you are using tinned chickpeas, drain them and cook the chopped vegetables in the liquid. Only add the chickpeas themselves at the last moment to heat them gently.

When the chickpeas are ready, boil a large quantity of water, add salt and then cook half the quantity of pasta. Break the remaining uncooked pasta into short pieces.

When the boiled pasta is nearly ready, heat some olive oil in a frying pan. Drain the boiled pasta, turn it into a large heated serving bowl, preferably earthenware, and add the cooked chickpeas, which should have absorbed most of the water and be in a thick, rich sauce. Stir well.

Now, at the last possible moment, fry the short lengths of pasta in the hot oil, stirring all the time with a wooden spoon. It will only take a few minutes for the pasta to swell, crisp and turn golden brown. Add this fried pasta and the olive oil to the serving bowl, mix well and serve immediately while the fried pasta is still very crunchy.

Minestra di Pasta e Ceci
PASTA AND CHICKPEAS

In the past this dish was served on days that the Church decreed *magro*, when meat was not to be eaten, and even today this dish is often eaten on Fridays, or the *vigilia*, the day before an important religious holiday.

300g/10oz dried pasta, preferably fettuccine, broken
into short lengths
300g/10oz dried chickpeas
1tsp chopped fresh rosemary leaves
4tbsp olive oil
2 garlic cloves, finely chopped
1 dried chilli pepper (optional)
2tbsp freshly made tomato sauce (optional, see page xxx)
salt and black pepper

Prepare the chickpeas as in the previous recipe. Put the drained chickpeas in a pan and cover with 1.5 litres/2½ pints cold water, add the rosemary, cover and cook gently until very soft. The traditional recipes specify 4 hours without removing the lid to check, but today's chickpeas rarely need more than 1 hour.

Heat the oil in a pan and gently cook the garlic and chilli until the garlic begins to change colour. Add the tomato sauce, if using, diluted with 125ml/4½fl oz boiling water. Purée half the chickpea mixture, then stir into the remaining chickpeas and cooking liquid. Stir in the tomato sauce and check the seasoning. Bring back to the boil and throw in the pasta. Cook until the pasta is soft then serve at once.

Note: If you are using pasta made without egg it will take longer to cook so stir the *minestra* from time to time to prevent it sticking to the bottom of the pan. This is a very thick *minestra* or broth. It is not usual to serve grated cheese with this dish.

Lampe e Tuone
LIGHTNING AND THUNDER

The name doubtless comes from the effect of the hot chilli and chickpeas on the digestion.

400g/14oz tagliatelle
300g/10oz dried chickpeas or 2 x 425g/15oz tins chickpeas
1tsp bicarbonate of soda
6tbsp olive oil
2 cloves garlic, chopped
3 litres/5 pints of boiling water

1tsp chopped fresh parsley
1tsp dried oregano
½ small hot chilli pepper, seeded and chopped or
1tsp dried chilli flakes
salt

Prepare the chickpeas as in the recipe for *Ciceri e Tria* (see page 40), drain and put in a saucepan with the oil and chopped garlic. Add 1 litre/1¾ pints of boiling water but no salt at this stage. Cook for about 2 hours until the chickpeas are tender, taking care not to let them boil dry. Add more boiling water if necessary.

When these chickpeas are just about ready (or if you are starting with tinned chickpeas), add the chopped parsley, oregano, chilli and salt to taste.

Transfer the chickpeas to a larger saucepan. Add the rest of the boiling water and when the mixture comes back to the boil, add the pasta. Cook until the pasta is ready, drain and serve immediately.

Pasta e Ceci
CHICKPEA AND PASTA BROTH

250g/9oz short pasta such as ditalini, or long pasta
broken into short lengths
300g/10oz dried chickpeas
1tsp bicarbonate of soda
2.5 litres/4 pints warm water
4 rashers streaky bacon, cut into strips
2 cloves garlic, chopped
2tbsp olive oil

230g/8oz tin Italian plum tomatoes, chopped
2 bay leaves
salt and freshly ground black pepper

Prepare the chickpeas as in the recipe for *Ciceri e Tria* (see page 40), then drain and put in a saucepan with the warm water.

Gently fry the bacon strips and garlic in 1 tablespoon of olive oil, then add the chopped tinned tomatoes and bay leaves. Add this mixture to the chickpeas. Cook slowly for about 2½ hours. Discard the bay leaves.

Purée half the chickpea mixture, then return to the remaining mixture in the saucepan. Bring back to the boil and add the pasta. Cook for a further 15 minutes. Add salt and pepper to taste and serve. Most Italians also add a spoonful of 'uncooked' olive oil at the table.

Continental or European Lentils
Lenticchie

These greeny brown lentils keep their shape when they are cooked and go very well with pasta. They make a tasty, nutritious cold-weather dish.

Lentils must first be washed under running water and any small stones or pieces of stalk removed. Then they must be soaked. If you have plenty of time, cover the lentils with twice their volume of cold water and leave for 12 hours. If you are in a hurry, you can speed up the process by putting them in a pan and covering them with cold water. Bring to the boil and cook for 5 minutes. Remove from the heat and leave to soak, covered, for 1 hour.

Pasta e Lenticchie
SMALL PASTA AND LENTIL BROTH

400g/14oz small pasta such as ditalini
300g/10oz green lentils, prepared as described
in the introduction
2tbsp olive oil
1 onion, chopped
1 stick celery, chopped
2 cloves garlic, chopped
1 small chilli pepper, chopped
500ml/16fl oz hot chicken stock
salt

Cook the prepared lentils in cold unsalted water for 30 minutes.

Heat the oil and gently fry the chopped vegetables and chilli pepper for about 5 minutes. Drain the lentils, return to the pan and add the hot stock and cooked vegetables. Cook for another 20 minutes, covered, on a low heat.

Now remove the lid and add the pasta. It should take about 10 minutes to cook. Have boiling water ready to add if the mixture becomes too dry. When ready, it should be a thick broth, in which, according to Italian tradition, one should be able to stand a spoon. Add salt to taste. Do not drain. Serve at once.

Note: In the Sicilian version of this dish the lentils are cooked and then processed to make a thick purée. The small pasta is cooked and drained, then mixed with the puréed lentils, black pepper and freshly grated Parmesan.

Courgettes
Zucchini

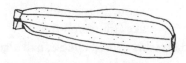

Twelve kilometres from Sorrento along a road winding past apricot-coloured houses and banks of bougainvillaea and hibiscus, a road with a spectacular close-up view of the island of Capri, we come to the small fishing village of Marina di Cantone. The last 9 kilometres of the precipitous road were finished only in 1960, and before this enthusiasts used to scramble down on foot, lured by thoughts of the local pasta speciality, Spaghetti Maria Grazia, made with slivers of courgettes and cheese.

My first recipe comes from the 'Maria Grazia' trattoria, which has been owned for generations by the Mellion family. From the outside it looks a little like a simple Greek taverna with its bright blue doors, pink-washed steps and white walls, and this impression is enhanced by the small white church, which is the top floor of the trattoria. However, the art of combining the spiritual and temporal, illustrated by the pink trattoria tablecloths drying on the balcony next to the small church bell tower, is wholly Italian.

The simple, functional terrace where swim-suited guests eat within a few feet of the sea, is open only at lunchtime, but the fame of the pasta speciality has attracted a sophisticated clientele, many of whom arrive by yacht or even small boats from Positano and other ports along the craggy Amalfi coast.

Spaghetti Maria Grazia
SPAGHETTI OF MARIA GRACE

500g/1lb spaghetti
2kg/4lb courgettes
150g/5oz freshly grated cheese, half Parmesan
and half pecorino
100g/4oz butter
a few basil leaves
freshly ground black pepper
oil, for deep frying

Choose small, tender courgettes and slice them finely in rounds without removing the skin. Heat a large quantity of oil and deep–fry the courgettes until they are a deep golden brown and have become somewhat crumpled. Remove from the pan, but allow them to retain a little oil. (This can be done well in advance.)

Cook the spaghetti in a large pan of boiling, salted water, following the packet directions very carefully to make sure you do not overcook the pasta.

While the pasta is cooking, gently warm the cooked courgettes in a pan. Divide the butter into small pieces and place in the serving bowl.

Drain the spaghetti when cooked, reserving 2 to 3 tablespoons of the water for the sauce. Gradually add the drained pasta to the butter in the serving bowl and add the reserved pasta water.

It helps at this stage if there is someone to help with adding the pasta since the spaghetti should be stirred all the time to melt the butter and coat every strand.

Now add the grated cheese and stir again until all the cheese has melted and a thick yellow cream is clinging to the spaghetti. Stir in the courgettes and mix very thoroughly to ensure an even distribution. Add freshly ground black pepper to taste and basil leaves if available. Stir once more and serve immediately.

Spaghetti con Zucchine
SPAGHETTI WITH COURGETTES

The traditional 'poor' version of spaghetti with courgettes, ideal for anyone avoiding animal fats, can be found throughout all the rural areas of Southern Italy where people have learned ways of making economical meals from their garden produce.

500g/1lb spaghetti
150ml/¼ pint olive oil
2kg/4lb tiny courgettes
freshly ground black pepper

Cook the pasta in a large pan of boiling, salted water. While it is cooking, slice the courgettes into thin rounds. Do not remove the skin. Fry them in hot olive oil until tender. When the pasta is cooked, drain it and stir in the courgettes and the olive oil in which they have been fried. Stir well, add black pepper to taste and serve. Cheese is not usually added to this dish.

Penne or Rigatoni con Zucchine
PENNE WITH COURGETTES, MOZZARELLA AND EGGS

500g/1lb penne or rigatoni
1kg/2lb courgettes
150ml/¼ pint olive oil
2 eggs
250g/9oz mozzarella, cubed
50g/2oz freshly grated Parmesan
freshly ground black pepper

Cut the courgettes into thin rounds, without peeling them and fry lightly in the olive oil. The courgette slices should be just tender and bright green, so take care not to overcook them. When they are ready, salt them and keep them warm. Keep the olive oil to add to the final dish.

Cook the pasta. Beat the 2 eggs together. Immediately the pasta is cooked, drain it and pour while still steaming hot into the heated serving bowl. Add the cubed mozzarella and stir swiftly so that the hot pasta starts to melt the cheese. Now add the eggs, courgettes and reheated olive oil, stirring quickly to set the eggs. Add the Parmesan and freshly ground black pepper to taste. Stir thoroughly and serve at once.

Pasticcio di Maccheroni con le Zucchine
BAKED PASTA WITH COURGETTES

500g/1lb short pasta such as farfalle or tortiglione
1kg/2lb courgettes
200ml/⅓ pint olive oil

50g/2oz butter
300g/10oz mozzarella
1 x quantity of tomato sauce (see page 90)

Preheat the oven to 220°C/425°F/gas 7. Cut the courgettes into thickish rounds, without peeling, and fry them lightly in the olive oil.

Cook the pasta in abundant boiling, salted water, for half the time stated on the packet. Drain, stir in the tomato sauce, add a knob of butter and mix well.

Butter a deep ovenproof serving dish and spread a thin layer of pasta at the bottom, then a layer of courgette slices, and cover these with thin slices of mozzarella. Repeat these layers until you have used up all your ingredients, finishing with a layer of mozzarella. Dot the top with the remaining butter and bake in the hot oven for 20 minutes until melted and golden brown. Serve hot.

Courgette Flowers
Fiori di Zucca

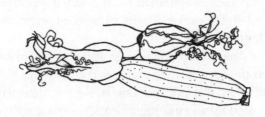

Courgette and other squash flowers are rarely seen for sale outside Italy. But there these spectacular yellow flowers are sold in bunches and are eaten either stuffed with anchovies and mozzarella cheese, dipped in batter and fried, or used to make deliciously different pasta sauces.

Here are two versions for keen gardeners who grow their own. The flowers need to be cooked when they are very fresh. The stalk, hairy pistil and stamens are removed and the flower is wiped with a moist piece of kitchen paper. It is too delicate to be washed in water.

Spaghetti ai Fiori di Zucca
SPAGHETTI WITH COURGETTE FLOWERS

500g/1lb spaghetti
4tbsp olive oil
3 cloves garlic, chopped

¼ small chilli pepper or ½tsp dried chilli flakes
8 courgette or squash flowers, chopped

Heat the oil and fry the chopped garlic and chilli pepper or flakes. Add the chopped courgette flowers and stir for 5 minutes, then keep warm.

Cook the spaghetti. Just before draining, reheat the sauce so that it is very hot. Remove the chilli pepper. Drain the pasta, pour over the sauce, stir quickly to coat every strand with oil and serve.

Vermicelli Abruzzesi
PASTA AND COURGETTE FLOWERS
FROM ABRUZZI

This recipe comes from the Abruzzi region in the middle of Italy, the centre of the saffron industry. It takes 130,000 crocus flowers to produce one kilo of saffron, which explains the high cost.

500g/1lb vermicelli or spaghetti
1tbsp olive oil
1 onion, chopped
1tsp saffron filaments or ¼ teaspoon saffron
powder, dissolved in a little hot stock
4tbsp chopped parsley
8 courgette or squash flowers, chopped
200ml/⅓ pint stock
1 egg yolk
40g/1½oz freshly grated Parmesan
salt and black pepper

Heat the oil and fry the onion gently until soft. Add the saffron, the parsley and the chopped courgette flowers. Cook for 10 minutes, then process or blend the mixture with the stock and return to the pan to keep warm.

Cook the pasta. Remove the sauce from the heat and add the egg yolk, freshly grated cheese and seasoning to taste. Stir well. Drain the pasta, pour on the sauce, mix thoroughly and serve.

Dried Beans
Fagioli

In Italy it is possible to buy beans that have been dried in their pods. The pods are a colourful combination of scarlet and cream streaks. These beans do not need soaking. However, during the winter dried beans as we know them are used. These can be bought by weight in the local market. Various qualities are displayed in their sacks and the careful shopper makes sure to choose fresh shiny beans. Those most commonly used for pasta are cannellini or borlotti.

Bucatini ai Fagioli
BUCATINI WITH BEANS

500g/1lb bucatini or spaghetti
150g/5oz dried beans
4tbsp olive oil

150g/5oz cooked ham or bacon, cut into matchsticks
1 clove garlic, finely chopped
parsley, finely chopped
sage, finely chopped
rosemary, finely chopped
1 small chilli pepper
60g/2½oz freshly grated Parmesan, pecorino
or similar cheese
salt

Soak the dried beans and drain, then cook in fresh water for about 1 hour. Heat the oil in another pan and add the ham or bacon and the finely chopped garlic and herbs. Cook for 5 minutes, then add the drained beans and the whole chilli pepper. Taste and add salt if necessary. Cook for 10 minutes, adding a little water if the mixture becomes too dry.

Meanwhile, cook the pasta, drain and turn into a heated serving bowl. Stir in the freshly grated cheese and then add the bean mixture. Remove the chilli pepper, stir well and serve at once.

Pasta e Fagioli
PASTA AND BEANS

This is a Neapolitan version of this popular combination.

400g/14oz mixed pasta or any short pasta
300g/10oz dried beans
4tbsp olive oil
2 cloves garlic, quartered
1 stick celery, chopped

230g/8oz tin Italian plum tomatoes, chopped
1tsp tomato paste
½ small chilli pepper
salt

Soak the dried beans for 10 hours or overnight. Drain, then cook in fresh water for about 1 hour.

While the beans are cooking, heat the oil and add the quartered garlic and chopped celery. When the garlic turns colour, remove it. Add the chopped tomatoes with their juice, tomato paste, chilli pepper, 100ml/3½fl oz water and salt to taste. Simmer for 10 minutes.

About 15 minutes before the beans are cooked, add the tomato mixture to the pan and cook together for the last 15 minutes. Remove the chilli.

A small quantity of beans and tomato are usually puréed to help the sauce coat the pasta. Return to the boil and add the pasta. Have boiling water ready to add if necessary but the finished dish should consist of almost 'dry' pasta in a thick sauce.

When the pasta is cooked, leave covered for 10 minutes, then serve.

Pasta e Fagioli
PASTA AND BEAN BROTH

This version, from Venice, is almost a broth.

300g/10oz tagliatelle
300g/10oz dried beans
200g/7oz bacon, chopped
1 ham bone, if available

6tbsp olive oil
1 onion, chopped
1 carrot, chopped
1 celery stick, chopped
salt and freshly ground black pepper
100g/4oz freshly grated Parmesan, to serve

Soak the dried beans for 10 hours or overnight. Drain, then put into a large saucepan with the bacon, ham bone, oil and chopped vegetables. Cover with cold water and simmer gently with the lid on for 2½ hours. Add salt to taste.

Remove the bone and purée half the mixture. Return the puréed mixture to the pan, bring back to the boil and add the pasta. When the pasta is cooking, check that you do not need to add boiling water, remembering that the finished dish will not be drained and should be a thick broth. Season with a little freshly ground black pepper and serve. The freshly grated Parmesan is usually served separately.

Garlic, Olive oil, Chilli
Aglio, olio e peperoncini

Many Italian dishes start with the winning combination of garlic, chilli pepper and olive oil, and every southern Italian kitchen has these in the larder. They make a basic sauce for pasta and you can add other favourite vegetables to make endless variations.

Spaghetti Aglio, Olio e Peperoncino
SPAGHETTI WITH GARLIC, OLIVE OIL
AND CHILLI PEPPER

This very basic sauce is traditionally served in the late, late hours, as an impromptu snack for anyone feeling pangs of hunger after the theatre or opera. Traditionally it is the elegant host who removes his jacket to prepare this instant nourishment for his guests, but it is my standby when I get home to an empty fridge, and it tastes just as good without the theatricals.

500g/1lb spaghetti
6tbsp olive oil
5 cloves garlic
1 small dried chilli pepper, broken into 2 or 4 pieces
1tbsp chopped parsley
wild rocket (optional)

In a large pan heat the olive oil and add the garlic. This is either left whole and removed before serving or it is finely chopped and not removed. Add the chilli pepper and cook until the garlic is golden brown. Meanwhile, cook the pasta, and the moment it is ready, stir it into the sauce. If you prefer you can remove the chilli but in Rome it is usually left in, and uninitiated guests told not to try to eat it. There must be sufficient sizzling oil to coat every strand of pasta and make it slippery and shiny. Today rocket seems to have taken over from parsley and it is wilted in the hot pasta just before serving.

Note: Another sauce can be prepared by altering the previous recipe as follows: replace the chilli with anchovy fillets, drained and chopped into small pieces; reduce the quantity of garlic to 2 cloves, left whole and removed once brown. Add 4 tablespoons of the pasta water to the finished dish and stir well.

Spaghetti Indiavolati
DEVILLED SPAGHETTI

This variation on oil, garlic and chilli gets its name from the small, very hot chilli peppers called *diavolicchi* – 'little devils'. A rather unusual method of infusion is used. The garlic and chilli are not fried and the final dish is lighter and more digestible.

500g/1lb spaghetti
6 cloves garlic
2 small very hot red chilli peppers
50g/2oz freshly grated Parmesan
3tbsp olive oil
parsley, to serve (optional)

Grind up the garlic and chillies in a blender with 500ml/16fl oz of water. Bring a large saucepan of salted water to the boil and add the mixture from the blender. Bring back to the boil and simmer gently for 15 minutes.

Pour the contents of the saucepan into another pan through a fine sieve and check to make sure that there is enough liquid to cook the pasta. If not, add more water. Discard the garlic and chillies.

Bring to the boil again and add the spaghetti. Cook carefully then drain and dress with the olive oil and the freshly grated cheese. Chopped parsley may be added if a touch of colour is desired.

Green Vegetables
La Verdura

There are many delicious sauces made using a mixture of green vegetables. Here are two of them. La Primavera is an extravagant recipe because it needs fresh young vegetables, which can be relatively expensive. Each vegetable has to be prepared separately to guarantee its perfection. However, it makes a spectacular first course for a spring dinner party and the vegetables can be prepared a little in advance.

Pasta alla Primavera
SPRING PASTA

500g/1lb tagliolini (tagliarini), green if available
12 spears tender young asparagus
200g/7oz fresh peas (the smaller the better), shelled
200g/7oz small broad beans, shelled or fine green beans
30g/1oz butter
200ml/⅓ pint double cream
60g/2½oz freshly grated Parmesan
salt and black pepper

Cook each vegetable separately in a small quantity of boiling salted water. It is better to slightly undercook because the vegetables must remain crisp and a good green colour. Drain and plunge immediately into cold water. Cut the tender part of the asparagus into 2cm/¾ inch lengths, discarding any tough parts. Remove the outer skin of the shelled broad beans. If you are substituting green beans, cut them into small lengths.

Heat the water for the pasta. Melt the butter in a small pan and as you add the pasta to the water add the various green vegetables to the butter. Stir for 2 minutes, then add the cream and pepper to taste and heat gently.

Drain the pasta and turn into a warmed serving dish. Toss thoroughly with the freshly grated cheese, then add the vegetables and cream. Stir to distribute the vegetables evenly and serve at once.

Pasta con la Verdura
PASTA WITH GREEN VEGETABLES

This recipe comes from the north of Italy – the Valtellina. Traditionally the pasta used for this hearty dish is made from buckwheat flour and known as '*pizzocheri*'. It can be bought dried in boxes but it works well with wholewheat pasta too.

500g/1lb tagliatelle, paglia e fieno or
fresh wholewheat ribbon pasta
3 medium potatoes, cut into walnut-size pieces
250g/9oz broccoli, cut into thin spears or cauliflower,
separated into florets
4 small courgettes or green beans
500g/1lb fresh spinach leaves or Chinese
leaves or lettuce

30g/1oz butter
1 large onion, finely chopped
100g/4oz freshly grated fontina or Emmenthal

Preheat the oven to 220°C/425°F/gas 7.

Bring a pan of salted water large enough to take all the ingredients to the boil. Add the potatoes and cook for 10 minutes. Then add the broccoli or cauliflower, the small whole courgettes or green beans, and whichever green leaves you are using.

Meanwhile, in a small frying pan, melt the butter and add the onion. Cover and cook gently until soft.

Ten minutes after adding the last green vegetable to the pan, add the pasta, which will cook quickly. Have a large ovenproof serving dish ready.

Drain the pasta and green vegetables thoroughly in a very large sieve or colander. Place half the pasta and vegetables in the serving dish. Add a layer of half the onions and half the freshly grated cheese. Now add the rest of the pasta and vegetables and the rest of the onions and cheese. Heat in the oven for 5 minutes, then serve.

Lemons

Limone

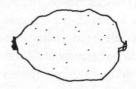

The first time I bought lemons with leaves it seemed to me a small miracle, and I get the same feeling every time I visit Amalfi, the famous lemon region, in the spring or summer months. The coastline is precipitous and the very narrow road has been carved out of the rock in an endless series of hairpin bends. There are tantalising glimpses of small churches with vivid mosaic domes, apricot- and peach-coloured houses covered with bougainvillaea, and the blue, blue sea. In the few places where the road widens, local women have set up their stalls to sell bunches of Amalfi lemons to the passers-by. These lemons are large and think-skinned, almost dimpled, and they are prized throughout Italy for their excellent flavour.

Linguine al Limone
LINGUINE WITH LEMON SAUCE

500g/1lb linguine or fine fresh pasta
2 large lemons
250ml/8fl oz double cream
100ml/3½fl oz grappa or acquavitae

Grate the zest from one of the lemons and put to one side. Remove and discard the white pith from the lemon and cut the fruit pulp into very small cubes. Squeeze the juice from the second lemon and keep separately.

Put the cream, lemon cubes and grappa into a pan and heat gently. Simmer until the sauce has become thicker.

Cook the pasta carefully following the packet directions to avoid overcooking. Remove the sauce from the heat and slowly add the lemon juice. Return to a low heat to cook for 1 minute, stirring all the time.

Now add 2 teaspoons of the grated lemon rind, stir well and pour over the drained pasta. Mix the sauce into the pasta and turn into a heated serving bowl. Put a few strands of lemon rind on top and serve.

Tagliolini al Limone
TAGLIOLINI WITH LEMON SAUCE

This sauce was created by Giuseppe Palladino for his lovely Roman restaurant, 'Vecchia Roma'.

500g/1lb tagliolini (tagliarini), preferably fresh
30g/1oz butter
1 clove garlic, finely chopped
1 very small piece of dried chilli pepper
zest of 2 lemons
100g/4oz cooked ham
500ml/16fl oz double cream
salt

Melt the butter and gently fry the garlic until it is golden brown. Add the chilli. Wash the lemons and grate the zest very finely, being sure not to grate the tough white skin as this will make the sauce bitter. If you use a zester, the fine threads of lemon can also serve as a garnish. Cut the ham into fine matchsticks, and add to the garlic and butter. Heat gently, then add the lemon zest and the cream. Simmer, uncovered, for just under 1 hour.

Heat a large pan of water and when it comes to the boil throw in the tagliolini. Drain it immediately because this process is not to cook the pasta, only to make it more flexible and less fragile.

Turn the sauce into a large pan and add the drained pasta. Cook gently for a very few minutes. Add salt to taste. If the sauce has become too dense, add a little more cream but be careful not to 'drown' the pasta. Turn into a heated serving dish, decorate the top with fine threads of lemon rind and serve at once.

Mushrooms
Funghi

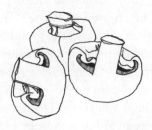

In Italian cooking, mushrooms in one form or another appear everywhere on the menu except the sweet course. They make light, tasty appetisers, delectable pasta sauces, a sumptuous main course – the great roast porcini mushrooms served whole in all their splendour – a refreshing, crisp salad ingredient, and sliced or *trifolato* as a harmonising accompaniment to meat or fish dishes.

The funghi porcini, or 'little pigs', are the most sought-after variety of mushroom. This is the cep or *boletus edulis*, which looks so repulsive but tastes so divine. In season they are displayed (uncooked) in local restaurants as a sort of Salvador Dali still life, and their high cost ensures that they are handled as reverently as a work of art. The waiters proudly exhibit them to the potential customer and the choice follows a painstaking inspection which is only equalled by the care with which an *inteditore*, or knowledgeable client, examines the gills and eyes of the fish on display before selecting what shall be cooked for him.

Out of season, dried porcini are used to make sauces and they prove a very acceptable substitute for fresh, especially in sauces with other ingredients. Packets of dried mushrooms are exported from Italy and may be used with confidence. Soak the dried mushrooms in tepid water for 15 minutes.

The pasta sauce, known as *carrettiere*, or 'carter's sauce', uses a very interesting combination of dried porcini, tomato and tuna fish and can be enjoyed at Rome's Trastevere restaurant, 'Checco er Carrettiere'. Checco, the grandfather of the present owner, Filippo Porcelli, used to drive his cart to the Castelli area outside Rome to transport wine back to the thirsty city. Today the 20-odd kilometres seem nothing to any Roman wanting to escape for an evening from Rome's torrid summer heat, but by horse and cart it was an arduous journey, especially when laden down by great quantities of wine. Grandmother Margherita thought up the following recipe as a sustaining one-course meal for the men of her family.

Spaghetti alla Carrettiere
CARTER'S STYLE SPAGHETTI

500g/1lb spaghetti or tagliatelle
250g/9oz mushrooms, fresh or dried
3tbsp olive oil
2 cloves garlic
1 small dried chilli pepper, broken into pieces or
1tsp crushed dried chilli flakes
100g/4oz bacon, cut into small cubes
400g/14oz tinned Italian plum tomatoes
80g/3oz tinned tuna, well-drained and flaked
chopped parsley, to serve

Wipe fresh mushroom caps with a damp cloth and slice finely, or soak dried mushrooms, drain and slice. Heat the oil and add the garlic and chilli pepper. When the garlic begins to change colour, add the bacon. When the fat begins to melt from the bacon, add the mushrooms and, after 5 minutes, the tomatoes. After 15 minutes on a low heat add the tuna fish. Cook gently for another 15 minutes.

During this time, cook the pasta carefully, following packet directions to avoid overcooking. Drain, turn into a heated serving dish and stir in the mushroom sauce, mixing well. Add the chopped parsley and serve at once.

Tagliatelle alla Boscaiola
FORESTER'S STYLE TAGLIATELLE

Any Italian dish with the name *boscaiola* includes mushrooms in some form.

500g/1lb tagliatelle or spaghetti
3tbsp olive oil
3 cloves garlic, finely chopped
400g/14oz tinned Italian plum tomatoes
300g/10oz fresh funghi porcini or dried equivalent
1tbsp chopped parsley
salt and black pepper

Heat two-thirds of the olive oil and add the finely chopped garlic. When it begins to turn colour, add the tomatoes with their juice, squashing them with a wooden spoon. Add salt and pepper to taste. Cook briskly for 15 minutes.

Meanwhile, heat the rest of the oil in a separate pan and add the mushrooms, which have been wiped with a damp cloth (or soaked in warm water for 15 minutes if using dried) and then finely sliced. Lightly salt the mushrooms and let them cook gently for 5 minutes. Add the chopped parsley and keep warm.

Cook the pasta, drain and stir into the tomato sauce, then add the mushrooms.

Bucatini con i Funghi
BUCATINI WITH MUSHROOMS

This dish can only be made with fresh mushrooms.

500g/1lb bucatini or spaghetti
1tbsp olive oil
2 cloves garlic, finely chopped
300g/10oz fresh mushrooms
1tbsp lemon juice
1tbsp chopped parsley
salt and black pepper

Heat the oil and add the garlic. Now add the mushrooms which have been wiped with a damp cloth and then finely sliced. Add a little seasoning, then cover the pan and leave to cook for 5 minutes over a low heat. The mushrooms should give out enough moisture to cook themselves gently. Cook the pasta.

Add the lemon juice and chopped parsley to the mushrooms then stir in the drained pasta. Serve at once.

Onions
Cipolle

Onions are used in conjunction with other ingredients in many pasta sauces but they also make a delicious sauce by themselves.

Tagliatelle con Cipolle
TAGLIATELLE WITH ONION SAUCE

500g/1lb tagliatelle
100g/4oz butter
500g/1lb onions, thinly sliced
chicken stock to cover
200ml/⅓ pint double cream
freshly grated nutmeg, to taste
freshly grated Parmesan (optional)
salt and black pepper

Melt the butter and cook the onions in a covered pan over a low heat until they are soft. Do not let them turn brown. Cover with chicken stock and simmer with the lid on for another 25 minutes. Purée the cooked onions and add the cream and salt, pepper and nutmeg to taste. Keep warm.

Cook the pasta, drain and pour into a heated serving bowl. Stir in the sauce. Freshly grated Parmesan may be served separately if desired.

Note: An even simpler version of this sauce can be made by omitting the cream and adding anchovies. The peeled onions are left under cold running water for 1 hour. They are then sliced and cooked as in the previous recipe, but the butter is replaced by 3 tablespoons of olive oil. Next, 6 finely chopped anchovy fillets are cooked slowly in the olive oil. While the pasta is cooking, the anchovies are added to the onions. In this recipe spaghetti or bucatini are usually used. After the pasta is drained, it is tossed in 50g/2oz of freshly grated Parmesan, then the sauce is stirred thoroughly into the pasta.

For another powerful onion sauce see also Rigatoni alla Genovese (page 137).

Tubetti 'Finta'
'FALSE' GENOVESE OR SHORT PASTA
WITH ONION SAUCE

This is the *'cucina povera'* version without the meat in the original 'Genovese' (see page 137).

500g/1lb tubetti or other short pasta
4tbsp extra virgin olive oil

1.5kg/3lbs onions, sliced thinly
200ml/⅓ pint light stock (optional)
100g/4oz freshly grated Parmesan
salt and black pepper

Heat the oil and stir in the onions with a little seasoning. Cover and cook very gently, gradually adding about 200ml/⅓ pint of hot water or light stock. Simmer for about 30 minutes, when the onion will be very soft and golden brown.

Cook the pasta in boiling, salted water. Drain, stir in half the cheese then the onion sauce. Sprinkle over the rest of the cheese and serve at once.

Pumpkin

Zucca

Autumn is the time of the year for pumpkin pasta dishes. They can be made with the beautiful, golden Cinderella-type pumpkin or with slices of the more prosaic green squashes. The sauce here has a very delicate flavour and it is very important to use good quality, freshly grated cheese. It is particularly delicious with fine, fresh pasta.

This recipe was given to me by Angelina Di Mambro of Ponte Milvio market in Rome. As she explained the recipe she cut up the pumpkin, leek and celery with lightning speed.

Tagliolini con la Zucca
PUMPKIN PASTA

1.5kg/3lb piece of pumpkin
50g/2oz butter
1 leek, finely chopped
1 stick celery, finely chopped
a little chicken stock
500g/1lb tagliolini (tagliarini) made with eggs, or
fine fresh pasta
150ml/¼ pint double cream, or 120g/4½oz fromage frais
80g/3oz freshly grated Parmesan
freshly grated nutmeg, to taste
salt and freshly ground black pepper

Peel the pumpkin and remove the seeds and any stringy fibres.
Cut the pumpkin into thin slices.

Melt half the butter and add the leek and celery to the pan.
Once they have softened, add the pumpkin slices and stir for a
few minutes. Now add a little stock and cover. Cook for about
20 minutes, adding more stock from time to time if necessary
to keep moist. Check the seasoning and add salt, freshly ground
black pepper and nutmeg to taste. Process the sauce in a blender
or food processor, then return to the pan and keep warm.

Cook the pasta carefully to avoid overcooking. Fresh pasta
will only need a few minutes, so add the cream to the sauce as
soon as you have thrown the pasta into the boiling water. Drain
the pasta and place in a heated dish. Stir in the freshly grated
cheese and then the pumpkin sauce. Mix well, add the rest of
the butter and serve at once.

Rocket
Rughetta or Rucola

In Italy, rocket can be found in every market in two versions
– wild and cultivated. The wild *rughetta* has spiky leaves and
a strong flavour, while the cultivated *rughetta* has larger leaves
and a milder taste. It is used in appetisers, pasta dishes, meat
dishes and salads.

If there is any *rughetta* and fresh Parmesan left over after
making pasta sauce, it is simple to produce a delicious side dish.
Wash and dry the rocket leaves, dress with a little olive oil and
then cover with fine shavings of Parmesan.

Pesto di rucola
PESTO WITH ROCKET

500g/1lb short pasta like penne or fusilli
2 cloves garlic, peeled
50g/2oz pine nuts or blanched almonds
4tbsp freshly grated Parmesan or 50g/2oz in pieces

100g/4oz cultivated rocket, washed and dried
100ml/3½fl oz extra virgin olive oil
salt and black pepper

Put the garlic, nuts and Parmesan in a food processor and process. Add the rocket and process some more, then slowly pour in the oil to make a smooth dressing. Season to taste. Cook the pasta, drain and stir in the sauce. You can add a ladle of pasta water if necessary.

Spaghetti con Pomodori e Rughetta
SPAGHETTI WITH FRESH TOMATOES
AND ROCKET

In summer, if you can get fresh plum tomatoes, you can make this unusual cold sauce.

500g/1lb spaghetti
300g/10oz ripe red plum tomatoes
4 cloves garlic, finely chopped
50g/2oz rocket, coarsely chopped
1½tbsp olive oil
salt and black pepper

Skin the tomatoes by first plunging them into boiling water for a few minutes. Chop finely and place in a large bowl together with the garlic and rocket. Add the olive oil and salt and pepper to taste and leave for at least 2 hours.

Cook the pasta as usual, drain and stir in the sauce.

Spinach
Spinaci

Washing fresh spinach has always been a rather tedious procedure, but it is now possible to buy bags of pre-washed spinach. In Italy it is usually washed in front of you if the market fountain is near enough, or else the stall lady – always the boss – orders her husband off to wash it for her!

Spinach plays three supporting roles with pasta: it is added to fresh pasta dough to give it a green colour; mixed with ricotta cheese to make a delicate filling for stuffed pasta; or used to make subtle, light sauces for cooked pasta.

Linguine con Salsa di Spinaci
LINGUINE WITH SPINACH

500g/1lb linguine or spaghetti
700g/1½lb fresh spinach leaves
40g/1½oz freshly grated Parmesan (optional)

for the béchamel sauce
60g/2½oz butter
60g/2½oz flour
500ml/16fl oz milk

freshly grated nutmeg, to taste
salt and black pepper

Wash the spinach. Finely chop a generous handful and put to one side. Cook the rest of the spinach very quickly in a covered saucepan. It will take about 5 minutes. Do not add any water, since the spinach will cook in the water remaining on the leaves after washing. Drain well, keeping the liquid to use later. Chop very finely and keep warm.

Make a béchamel sauce, using the butter, flour and milk, then dilute with the reserved spinach liquid. Check for seasoning and add a little grated nutmeg. Cook the pasta.

Add the cooked chopped spinach to the béchamel sauce and at the very last minute add the finely chopped raw spinach. This will make the sauce a more attractive green and improve the flavour. Pour onto the drained pasta, mix well and serve at once. Freshly grated Parmesan can be served separately, if desired.

Tagliatelle al Mascarpone e Spinaci
TAGLIATELLE WITH MASCARPONE
AND SPINACH

500g/1lb tagliatelle
20g/¾oz butter
1 clove garlic
300g/10oz fresh spinach leaves, finely chopped
150ml/¼ pint double cream
150g/5oz mascarpone cream cheese
a little chicken stock
black pepper

Melt the butter and add the garlic, whole, allowing it to turn golden brown. Add the spinach and cook over a low heat until tender. In a separate pan, put the cream and mascarpone, add a little stock to dilute and pepper to taste. Leave to simmer gently for a few minutes. Cook the pasta.

Remove the garlic from the spinach. Drain the pasta, turn into a warm serving bowl and add first the cream sauce and then the spinach. Stir well and serve at once.

Pasticcio di Maccheroni con Salsa Verde
BAKED PASTA SHELLS WITH A GREEN SAUCE

500g/1lb conchiglie
1kg/2lb fresh spinach leaves
100g/4oz butter
250ml/8fl oz chicken stock
100g/4oz freshly grated Parmesan
8tbsp toasted breadcrumbs
salt and black pepper

Preheat the oven to 220°C/425°F/gas 7. Wash the spinach and cook very quickly in a covered saucepan. It will take about 5 minutes. Do not add any water, since the spinach will cook in the water remaining on the leaves after washing. Drain well and chop finely.

Melt 20g/¾oz of the butter in a pan and add the chopped cooked spinach. Stir for about 5 minutes, then add the stock. Boil fiercely to reduce the sauce, then add seasoning to taste and 80g/3oz of the cheese. You should now have a thick, creamy sauce.

Cook the pasta for 5 minutes less than stated in the instructions on the packet. Just before it's ready to take off the heat, melt 60g/2½oz of the butter in a pan. Drain the pasta and toss in the melted butter.

Butter a deep oven dish and make alternate layers of pasta and green sauce, finishing with a pasta layer. Cover with the toasted breadcrumbs mixed with the remaining cheese. Dot with the rest of the butter and add pepper to taste. Bake in the hot oven for 10 minutes, finishing under a hot grill if necessary.

Sweet Peppers
Peperoni

The rather sweet, large, shiny red and yellow peppers are used in preference to green in pasta sauces.

In Italy, peppers are usually skinned because the skin is thought to be indigestible and bitter in taste. Place the peppers under a very hot grill and turn them until all the skin is uniformly black. The skin can then be peeled off quite easily and the pepper itself remains firm. The peppers can also be skinned after being roasted in a hot oven.

Penne con Peperoni
QUILLS WITH SWEET PEPPER SAUCE

This pasta recipe was first cooked for me in Acquaviva in Castro, Puglia. The Salento peninsula seems to produce very individual recipes and the smell of this little-known pepper sauce conjures up visions for me of the small natural harbour, the rocky coastline and the winding road leading up to the castle and fortified old town of Castro, believed to be the Castrum Minervae of Virgil's *Aeneid*.

500g/1lb penne or other short pasta
1kg/2lb sweet red and yellow peppers
4tbsp olive oil
4 cloves garlic, chopped
1tbsp chopped parsley
salt

Remove the seeds and fibres from the peppers and cut them into strips about the same size as the pasta. Heat the oil, add the garlic and when it begins to turn colour add the peppers. Cover and cook gently for 10 minutes. Remove the lid and turn up the heat. Cook for another 5 minutes. Add salt to taste.

Cook the pasta, drain, turn into a heated serving bowl and stir in the pepper mixture and the chopped parsley. Serve at once.

Spaghetti Siracusani
SPAGHETTI SYRACUSE

Named after the Sicilian town of Syracuse, this is again made from ingredients usually found in every Italian kitchen.

500g/1lb spaghetti or short pasta if preferred
1 large aubergine, sliced, put under salt then diced
2tbsp extra virgin olive oil
3 garlic cloves, chopped
4 anchovy fillets, chopped

4 large red tomatoes, skinned and chopped or
230g/8oz tin plum tomatoes, chopped
2tbsp capers, rinsed and chopped
12 black olives, pitted and chopped
2 sweet peppers, seeded and cut into small strips
fresh basil leaves
2tbsp freshly grated pecorino
salt

Cut the aubergine into medium-thick slices and leave to 'purge' (see page 15), then rinse, dry with a paper towel and cut into dice. Heat the olive oil and add the aubergine, garlic, anchovies, and tomatoes. Cook gently for 10 minutes, then add the capers, olives, peppers and basil. Cover and cook gently for about 15 minutes. Add salt to taste.

Cook the pasta; drain. Stir the sauce into the pasta, add the pecorino and serve at once.

Linguine con Peperoni
LINGUINE WITH SWEET PEPPER

500g/1lb linguine or spaghetti
2½tbsp olive oil
3 cloves garlic, roughly chopped
1 onion, roughly chopped
6 large sweet red and yellow peppers, seeds and
coarse fibres removed, roughly chopped
salt

Heat the oil and add the roughly chopped garlic and onion, then add the peppers. Add a little salt and stew in a covered pan over a low heat for 2 hours. (I prefer to do this in an earthenware pot in the oven.) The peppers will produce their own liquid and practically melt into the sauce.

Pass the mixture through a sieve or the fine blade of a food mill. (A blender or processor does not produce the same effect.) Keep the sauce warm.

Cook the pasta, drain and turn into a heated serving bowl. Stir in the sauce and serve at once.

Note: A similar sauce can be made using 2 red, 2 yellow and 2 green peppers, and half the quantity of oil. After the peppers are passed through the food mill, a little cream is stirred into the sauce before it is added to the pasta.

Tomato
Pomodoro

Hard though it is to imagine Italy without the tomato, the fruit was only brought to Europe in the sixteenth century from voyages of discovery to Mexico and Peru. Because its iron and vitamin content was seen to impart a lusty vigour, the tomato was first known as *pomme d'amour* or 'love apple'. The name eventually became changed to *pomme d'or* or 'golden apple', evoking memories of the Hesperides myth, and in Italy the name *pomodoro* is still used today.

During the summer one can find at least four types of tomatoes in local markets in Italy. The unripe orangey-green tomatoes are preferred for salad while the large, round red tomatoes are used mainly stuffed with rice. The tomato used for sauce is the San Marzano, the plum tomato that is also tinned and exported all over the world. In the south, the small round cherry tomato is also used for a pasta sauce.

Even in the cities the Italian housewife buys fresh tomatoes daily throughout the summer to make her sauce. In September, large crates of tomatoes (popularly known as *oro rosso* or 'red gold') are sold by the roadside and every Fiat seems in danger of being crushed under the weight of the crates of tomatoes stacked on top. The great task of making enough bottled tomatoes to last the winter begins. Whole families – grandparents, fathers, mothers, children – gather together to help in the yearly ritual. The washed tomatoes are put through a simple apparatus that removes the skin and seeds. The resulting purée is poured into clean beer or mineral water bottles, and usually a leaf or two of basil is added before the bottles are capped and sterilised in a seething cauldron of boiling water. This procedure is nearly always carried out in the open air and driving through the countryside one comes upon small, brilliant red 'rivers' where the grass and earth have been stained with the huge quantity of skins and seeds thrown out by the primitive pulping machines. This filtered purée is known as *passato* and even today, when it can be bought already bottled, a large proportion of the populace take pride and pleasure in this personal replenishment of the storecupboard.

In Puglia and Magna Grecia, the ancient method of drying tomatoes in the hot southern sun is still used. These dried tomatoes can be bought in small glass jars in speciality shops. They have a very strong, concentrated flavour and are perhaps an acquired taste.

Tinned, peeled tomatoes known as *pelati* are also used to make pasta sauce and are the first resort of most cooks outside Italy. The hot sun gives a unique flavour to Italian tomatoes. Even the same variety grown in northern climates would not have the same taste and it would be a mistake to try to use them for pasta sauces. Always use tinned Italian tomatoes in preference to a fresh northern variety. If you do happen to have fresh plum tomatoes, remove the skins by plunging them into boiling water for a few minutes. Allow slightly less cooking time because there will be less liquid to evaporate.

There are many different versions of tomato sauce and every Italian family has its own favourite. Some prefer to leave the garlic and onion whole, removing the garlic at the end of the frying time and the onion before sieving the final sauce. (The onion is then usually much in demand as a tasty titbit!) Some cooks add a small piece of celery, finely chopped, with the onion and garlic, others add celery and chopped carrot. I have known families who add a good spoonful of brandy to the nearly-finished sauce (rather like the Italian habit of adding brandy, or other liqueurs, to their morning black espresso coffee, which is then called *caffè coretto* or 'corrected coffee'!), while others content themselves with adding a generous dose of good red wine.

No two tomato sauces are ever identical. This is generally accepted, and in Sicily there is even an expression to describe a changeable personality: *Cambia sempre come la salsa* – 'He is always different, like a sauce'.

BASIC TOMATO SAUCE

2tbsp extra virgin olive oil
1 small onion, finely chopped
2 cloves garlic, finely chopped
1kg/2lb ripe tomatoes or 2 x 400g/14oz tins peeled
Italian plum tomatoes
2tbsp fresh basil, torn
salt and pepper

Heat the oil and gently cook the onion and garlic until soft. Add the tomatoes and basil, then cook quickly until most of the juice has evaporated. If you want to keep the good red colour ,put through a food mill as tomatoes turn orange when a blender or food processor is used.

Tagliatelle o Spaghetti al Pomodoro
TAGLIATELLE OR SPAGHETTI WITH TOMATO SAUCE

500g/1lb tagliatelle or spaghetti
2tbsp olive oil
1 medium onion, chopped
2 cloves garlic, chopped
2 x 400g/14oz tins Italian plum tomatoes
1tsp sugar
60g/2½oz freshly grated Parmesan
salt and freshly ground black pepper

Heat the oil and gently fry the onion and garlic until softened. I usually cover the pan to prevent browning. Add the tomatoes with their juice, sugar, salt and freshly ground pepper to taste and cook on a high heat, uncovered, for about 20 minutes, stirring occasionally. When the sauce is reduced and thick, check the seasoning, then pass the sauce through the medium disc of a food mill. (Although not authentic, you can also use an electric blender or food processor to save time.)

Cook the pasta, drain and add half the freshly grated cheese, stirring thoroughly. Then add the sauce. Stir well, add the rest of the cheese and serve.

Tagliatelle al Pomodoro e Basilico
TAGLIATELLE WITH TOMATO AND BASIL

This sauce is only worth making if you have fresh basil. Basil leaves lose much of their perfume if they are washed in water; they should just be wiped gently with a piece of slightly moist kitchen paper.

500g/1lb tagliatelle or spaghetti
2tbsp olive oil
2 x 400g/14oz tins Italian plum tomatoes
8 basil leaves
salt and black pepper
40–60g/1½–2½oz freshly grated Parmesan (optional)

Heat the oil and add the tomatoes with their juice, squashing them in the pan with a fork. Cook rapidly for 5 or 10 minutes, no longer, to retain the fresh vivid red colour. Add salt and pepper to taste and the whole basil leaves. Stir well.

Cook the pasta in boiling salted water, drain the moment it is ready, add the sauce, toss and serve.

This sauce is usually served without cheese, but if you like, add the freshly grated Parmesan to the pasta and stir thoroughly before you add the sauce.

Penne all'Arrabbiata
PASTA QUILLS WITH FIERY SAUCE

This sauce seems to have developed in the 1940s and is believed to owe its origin to Italy's Libyan campaign and the soldiers' introduction to hot, peppery Arab cooking.

500g/1lb dry penne or spaghetti
1 x quantity of tomato sauce (see page 90)
1 small chilli pepper, chopped, or 1tsp dried chilli flakes
2tbsp chopped fresh parsley

Make the tomato sauce, adding the chopped chilli pepper to the garlic and onions and frying gently before adding the tomatoes. Traditionally, quill-shaped pasta, such as penne is used, but the sauce goes well with any packet pasta. It is not good with fresh pasta. Add the chopped parsley before serving. Cheese is not usually served with this sauce.

Note: Some versions of this 'rabid' sauce include 120g/4½oz bacon in the initial frying, but I prefer the tangy, healthy Roman version with no animal fat.

Spaghettini con Pomodorini Pachino
SPAGHETTINI WITH PACHINO CHERRY TOMATOES

In the past in winter everyone in Rome used bottled or tinned tomatoes for their pasta sauces when the San Marzano plum tomatoes were unavailable. (It is better to use good, full-taste tinned tomatoes than insipid tasting fresh tomatoes.) Then eating habits were revolutionised by the advent of a small, sweet winter tomato from Pachino in Sicily. They are vine ripened and sold with stalks still intact. The perfume that is released as the stalks are removed signals their very special flavour. These tomatoes are usually served southern-style, without the skins being removed, and the taste is so intense the pasta is usually served without any cheese. Only try this recipe with the full-flavour small tomatoes.

400g/14oz spaghettini or other dried pasta
3tbsp extra virgin olive oil
1 small onion, chopped
500g/1lb small full-flavour tomatoes, cut into halves
6 fresh basil leaves
salt and black pepper

Put the pasta on to cook. Heat the oil, add the onions and let them soften and begin to change colour before adding the tomatoes. Leave them on a low heat for just a few minutes because you do not want the skins to come off. Add the whole basil leaves and seasoning, then drain the al dente pasta and stir into the tomatoes.

Pesto Trapanesi
PASTA WITH TOMATO AND ALMOND PESTO

In Trapani, in Sicily, this dish is usually made with a flour-and-water home-made pasta called *busiati*. I prefer to use a thin, short dry pasta like *mezza zita tagliata* or *piccole penne*. It is only prepared in the summer with ripe, red tomatoes. Traditionally mint is used, which gives an intriguing 'new' taste, but some families prefer to use basil.

500g/1lb short dried pasta
8 large red tomatoes
40g/1½oz blanched almonds
4 cloves garlic, peeled
100g/4oz mint leaves or basil leaves
4tbsp extra virgin olive oil
salt and black pepper

Plunge the tomatoes into boiling water for a few minutes, remove with a slotted spoon, peel off the skins and cut into quarters. Place the almonds in a food processor and chop roughly, then add the garlic, mint or basil and salt. Chop until they resemble coarse breadcrumbs. Now pour in the oil, process, then add the tomatoes. It is important not to over-process. There should be a slightly gritty texture. This sauce can be prepared in advance. When ready to eat, bring a large pot of water to a brisk boil, add some coarse salt and throw in the pasta. When it is still al dente, drain and stir in enough of the pesto sauce to coat the pasta. There should not be extra sauce left in the bottom of the serving bowl.

Spaghetti Sorrentina o Vesuviano
SPAGHETTI WITH SORRENTINA OR VESUVIANO SAUCE

500g/1lb spaghetti
1 x quantity fresh tomato sauce (see page 90)
60g/2½oz freshly-grated Parmesan
200g/7oz mozzarella, diced
5 or 6 basil leaves, roughly torn into pieces
coarse sea salt

Make the tomato sauce and put to one side. Bring a large pan of water to the boil and add a handful of coarse salt. Throw in the pasta and bring back to a fierce boil. When the pasta is nearly ready, reheat the tomato sauce. Drain the pasta and, working quickly, stir in the Parmesan, tomato sauce, mozzarella and basil. Toss rapidly, then cover for 2 minutes so that the mozzarella begins to melt and look like molten lava from Vesuvius. Serve at once.

Rigatoni al Forno con Salsa Aurora
BAKED RIGATONI WITH AURORA SAUCE

'Rosy-fingered Dawn', beloved of the Latin poets, gives her name to this recipe.

500g/1lb rigatoni or other short pasta
250ml/8fl oz tomato sauce (see page 90)
125g/4oz freshly grated Parmesan
8tbsp toasted breadcrumbs
30g/1oz butter
salt and freshly ground black pepper

for the béchamel sauce
80g/3oz butter
90g/3½oz flour
700ml/1¼ pints milk
freshly grated nutmeg, to taste
salt and black pepper

Preheat the oven to 220°C/425°F/gas 7. Make a béchamel sauce using the butter, flour, milk and seasonings. Stir in the tomato sauce. Check for seasoning and add salt and freshly ground pepper if needed.

Cook the pasta for half the time given in the packet directions, drain and mix well with the sauce and half the freshly grated cheese. Turn into a buttered oven dish and cover with the rest of the grated cheese mixed with the breadcrumbs. Dot with the remaining butter.

Bake in the hot oven for 10 minutes. If a browner crust is desired, place under a hot grill for a few minutes.

Penne al Forno con Pomodoro e Mozzarella
BAKED PENNE WITH TOMATO AND CHEESE

500g/1lb penne or other short pasta
1 x quantity of tomato sauce (see page 90)
50g/2oz freshly grated Parmesan
300g/10oz mozzarella cheese
8tbsp toasted breadcrumbs

Preheat the oven to 220 °C/425 °F/gas 7. Cook the pasta for half the time given in the packet directions and drain. Put 125ml/4½fl oz of the tomato sauce to one side and mix the rest with the pasta. Add one third of the freshly grated Parmesan.

Butter an oven dish and put in half the pasta. Cover with thin slices of mozzarella, the reserved tomato sauce and half the remaining Parmesan. Add the rest of the pasta and cover with the remaining Parmesan mixed with the breadcrumbs. Bake in the hot oven for 20 minutes.

Walnuts
Noci

Walnuts go very well with pasta and cheese, and in Liguria it is customary to serve a walnut sauce with the herb and vegetable-stuffed pasta *pansooti* or ravioli. The sauce is very rich so if you are making this for a first course serve about six spinach and ricotta ravioli per person.

Ravioli con Salsa di Noci
RAVIOLI WITH WALNUTS SAUCE

36 ravioli or other pasta stuffed with spinach
and ricotta (6 per person)
200g/7oz shelled walnuts
200ml/⅓ pint good quality olive oil
50g/2oz butter
50g/2oz freshly grated Parmesan
100ml/3½fl oz double cream
salt

This speedy sauce can be made in advance or while the pasta is cooking, whichever you prefer. Chop the nuts in a food processor, then add the olive oil and butter. Next add the grated cheese, cream and salt to taste.

Cook the pasta, drain and coat with the sauce. I prefer to serve directly onto individual plates to avoid squashing the rather delicate cooked pasta.

Tagliatelle con Salsa di Noci
TAGLIATELLE WITH WALNUTS
AND MASCARPONE

500g/1lb tagliatelle
50g/2oz butter
1 clove garlic, finely chopped
200g/7oz shelled walnuts
200g/7oz mascarpone or cream cheese
60g/2½oz freshly grated Parmesan

Melt the butter and fry the finely chopped garlic until it is golden brown. Chop the nuts finely in a food processor and add to the garlic and butter, stir for 3 minutes then remove from the heat.

Cook the pasta carefully to avoid over cooking. Add the cream cheese to the nuts and heat gently. Drain the pasta, toss in the grated Parmesan and transfer to a heated serving dish. Stir in the sauce and serve at once.

FISH SAUCES

Fish

Pesce

Linguine al Tonno, Limone e Rughetta
LINGUINE WITH TUNA, LEMON AND ROCKET

The tuna is still fished off the south coast of Italy and the whole bloody ritual of the great kill, the *tonnara*, with its Arabic terms and stylised movements, follows age-old custom. Those helping to trap and kill the fish were rewarded with a large piece of tuna and, before widespread refrigeration, the fish was preserved under olive oil. This is what is traditionally used for tuna pasta sauces.

Over the years this has gradually become one of my favourite pasta dishes and we eat it all through the year. In Rome we can buy small bunches of wild rocket that has a pungent flavour, much stronger than cultivated rocket. Although the *'ventresca'* is usually considered the best cut of tuna, I find it easier to stir in the smaller flakes to get a more even distribution through the pasta. Therefore I use a cheaper cut, but for the flavour it is important to use tuna preserved in olive oil.

400g/14oz linguine
3tbsp extra virgin olive oil
2 garlic cloves, finely chopped
1 dried red chilli pepper, broken into 2 or 3 pieces
200g/7oz tin tuna in olive oil, drained and flaked
juice of 2 lemons
a large bunch of fresh rocket leaves, roughly chopped

Heat the oil and gently cook the garlic and chilli pepper. As the garlic begins to change colour add the tuna and stir around the pan. Remove from the heat.

Cook the pasta, drain when still slightly hard and stir into the tuna mixture. Squeeze over the lemon juice and add the rocket. Using a wooden fork, lift up the pasta and really keep turning it over so that the rocket wilts and the tuna is evenly distributed and not left at the bottom of the pan. Serve at once.

Linguine al Tonno e Pomodoro
LINGUINE WITH TUNA AND TOMATO

500g/1lb linguine or spaghetti
2tbsp olive oil
1 medium onion, chopped
2 cloves garlic, chopped
2 x 400g/14oz tins Italian plum tomatoes
200g/7oz tin tuna, drained and flaked
2tbsp chopped capers (optional)
4tbsp chopped fresh parsley
salt and black pepper

Heat the oil and gently fry the onion and garlic until softened. Add the tomatoes with their juice and salt and pepper to taste and cook on a high heat for 10 minutes, stirring occasionally. Purée in a food mill, blender or food processor and return to the pan. Add the tuna and capers, if using, and cook for a further 10 minutes.

Cook the pasta, drain and add the sauce. Stir well and add the chopped parsley. Cheese is not served with this recipe.

Linguine 'Vecchia Marina'
LINGUINE WITH SWORDFISH
AND COURGETTE

This recipe comes from the 'Vecchia Marina' restaurant in Cefalu in Sicily. It has a terrace overlooking the sea and since the kitchen enjoys the same view, the chef is inspired when he cooks seafood. The Sicilian use of mint and pine nuts gives this dish an extra dimension.

500g/1lb linguine
3tbsp extra virgin olive oil
4 courgettes, diced
2tbsp pine nuts
1 small onion, finely chopped
2 garlic cloves, finely chopped
250g/9oz swordfish, diced
3tbsp chopped fresh mint
3tbsp dry white wine (optional)
4 ripe tomatoes, chopped
salt and black pepper

Heat 1 tablespoon of the oil and fry the diced courgettes. As they begin to turn colour add the pine nuts and cook until golden brown. Remove from the pan and set the mixture aside. Add another tablespoon of oil to the pan, add the onion and garlic and let them soften without changing colour. Add the remaining oil and stir in the swordfish and mint. After a few minutes pour in the wine, if using, then stir in the tomatoes and courgette mixture, season to taste and set to one side. Cook the pasta in boiling, salted water, drain and stir into the sauce. Serve at once.

Bucatini al Sugo di Pesce
PASTA WITH FISH SAUCE

This dish from Campania is made with the great red *scorfano* or *rascasse* (scorpion fish), which gives Mediterranean fish soups their inimitable flavour. When combined with pasta it makes a wonderfully satisfying one-pot meal.

500g/1lb bucatini, linguine or perciatelli
1 scorfano fish, weighing approx. 1kg/2lb, scaled and gutted
3tbsp extra virgin olive oil
1 small onion, finely sliced
2 cloves garlic, peeled
6 basil leaves
3tbsp dry white wine
700g/1½lb Italian plum tomatoes, peeled,
chopped and sieved
salt and black pepper

Rinse the fish and put to drain with the head hanging down.

Heat the oil and gently cook the onion and garlic until very soft. Add the basil then place the whole fish in the pan, turning it over so that each side cooks gently. Add the wine a little at a time. When this has nearly evaporated pour in the sieved tomatoes and season to taste. Cover and cook gently for about 30 minutes.

Lift the fish from the sauce, removing the head, skin and bones. Discarding the garlic and basil, flake the fish and return it to the sauce. Keep warm.

Cook the pasta, drain and stir in the sauce. Serve at once.

Spaghetti con Acciughe in Salsa di Arancia
SPAGHETTI WITH ANCHOVIES AND
ORANGE SAUCE

I first ate this in Calabria at the restaurant 'Alia'. In Sicily oranges are often used with fish, but this is an unusual combination for the mainland.

500g/1lb spaghetti
200g/7oz anchovy fillets in oil, cut into small pieces
or anchovies in salt
2tbsp olive oil
1 garlic clove, finely chopped
2 oranges, peeled and cubed
1tbsp fresh breadcrumbs
3tbsp orange liqueur
1tbsp chopped fresh mint
salt

If you are using anchovies in salt you need to wash well and remove the central bone, then cut the fish into small pieces.

Heat the oil and gently cook the garlic until it begins to change colour. Now add the anchovies, pushing them down with a wooden spoon until they 'melt' and form a thick cream.

Add the orange cubes to the anchovies together with the breadcrumbs and the liqueur,

Taste to see if more salt is needed. Cook the pasta, drain and stir in the sauce. Sprinkle with the chopped mint and serve at once.

SHELLFISH SAUCES

Shellfish
Frutti di Mare

Italy has a long coastline and every Italian loves to eat seafood. When the Church abolished the compulsory fish day on Friday, people continued to follow tradition and every trattoria serves a shellfish pasta on Fridays.

Linguine alle Cozze
LINGUINE WITH MUSSELS

500g/1lb linguine
500g/1lb mussels, scrubbed and de-bearded
3tbsp extra virgin olive oil
2 garlic cloves, finely chopped
1 dried red chilli pepper, crushed
a splash of white wine
2tbsp finely chopped parsley, to serve
salt

Put the mussels with a little water into a large, covered pan. Heat fiercely so that the shells open. Discard any mussels that have failed to open. Remove most of the mussels from the shell, but keep a few intact for their aesthetic value.

Heat the oil and gently cook the garlic and chilli pepper. As the garlic begins to change colour add the mussels and splash with white wine. Cook the pasta in boiling, salted water, drain when still slightly hard and stir into the pan with the mussels. Turn up the heat. Shake the pan, sprinkle with parsley and serve at once.

Linguine alle Mazzancolle
LINGUINE WITH PRAWNS

500g/1lb linguine
2tbsp extra virgin olive oil
2 garlic cloves, finely chopped
1cm/½ inch square fresh ginger, peeled and grated (optional)
1 dried chilli pepper, crushed
1kg/2lb large prawns, shelled and cleaned, 8 left
whole, the rest cut into 2 or 3 large pieces
1tbsp lemon juice
a large glass of dry white wine
1 handful wild rocket
salt

In a large pan heat the oil and gently cook the garlic, ginger and chilli pepper. When the garlic begins to change colour, add all the prawns and stir-fry for a few minutes before adding a little salt and the lemon juice. Pour in the wine and let it bubble. Cook the linguine in boiling salted water until very al dente, drain and stir in the sauce. Simmer for a further 3 minutes, while shaking the pan, add the rocket, let it wilt, stir and serve.

Spaghetti alle Vongole
SPAGHETTI WITH CLAMS

Roman trattorias have taken this dish to their heart, and it is probably on every menu on Fridays, and quite frequently on other days too. The best clam is the *vongole verace*, but smaller clams are often substituted. The sauce is so good there is even a 'poor', clamless version, with the *vongole* still at sea!

500g/1lb spaghetti
1kg/2lb vongole verace in shell, scrubbed thoroughly
4tbsp extra virgin olive oil
2 garlic cloves, chopped
1 chilli pepper, crushed
a small glass of white wine
2tbsp chopped fresh parsley

Place the clams in a pan with 100ml/3½fl oz of water and leave on a high heat until the clams open. Discard any clams that fail to open, strain the cooking liquid and put to one side.

In a large pan heat the oil and gently cook the garlic and chilli pepper. When the garlic starts to turn colour, stir in the clams in their shells and pour over the reserved cooking water. Add the wine and simmer for a few minutes. Keep warm.

Cook the pasta in lightly salted boiling water, drain and stir into the clams. Add the parsley, stir well and serve.

Tagliatelle con Capesante
TAGLIATELLE WITH SCALLOPS

500g/1lb tagliatelle
6tbsp olive oil
1 leek, finely sliced
300g/10oz scallops, shelled and cut into 3 or 4 pieces
a small glass of dry white wine
salt and black pepper

Heat half the oil and gently cook the leek, adding a little water if it gets too dry. Heat the remaining oil and cook the scallops, splashing with the white wine. Add the scallops and their cooking liquid to the leeks so that the flavours amalgamate, and season to taste. Cook the tagliatelle in boiling, salted water, drain and stir in the sauce. Add more black pepper and serve at once.

Spaghetti con Polpa di Granchio
SPAGHETTI WITH CRAB MEAT AND SAFFRON

This pasta can be prepared with any crab meat, and the saffron adds an intriguing touch of colour.

500g/1lb spaghetti
2tbsp extra virgin olive oil
1 onion, finely chopped
250g/9oz crab meat
a splash of dry white wine

a little saffron (powder or filaments)
1tbsp chopped fresh parsley
salt and black pepper

Heat the oil and gently soften the onion. Add the crab meat to warm through and then the white wine and seasoning. Dissolve the saffron in a little warm water and stir into the pan so that the crab meat takes on a golden hue. Cook the pasta in boiling, salted water, drain and stir in the crab sauce and a little chopped parsley. Serve at once.

CHEESE SAUCES

Cheese

Formaggio

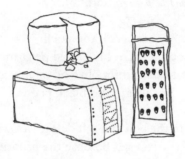

In pasta dishes, the most important cheese is Parmesan. In Italy it is regarded as one of the necessities of life, even mentioned by Boccaccio in the *Decameron*. Parmesan must be bought in the piece and always grated just before use. It keeps very well wrapped tightly in foil in the refrigerator. Do not be tempted to use ready-grated Parmesan. If you do not have any fresh Parmesan to hand, it is better to use a freshly grated substitute cheese or switch menus.

Pecorino is a more pungent cheese reserved for the more robust sauces. Parmesan can be used in place of pecorino if the latter proves difficult to find, but never substitute pecorino for Parmesan. The taste is too strong for many of the more delicate sauces.

Tonarelli Cacio e Pepe
PASTA WITH PECORINO CHEESE AND
BLACK PEPPER

This is a very simple, quick 'Roman' recipe which can be prepared with any pasta, although tonnarelli seem to work best. It belongs to the *cucina povera* tradition.

500g/1lb tonnarelli
100g/4oz freshly grated pecorino
2tbsp good extra virgin olive oil or 30g/1oz butter
freshly ground black pepper

Bring the water to the boil and salt before throwing in the pasta. For this recipe I use less salt because the pecorino is very salty. Grate the pecorino as the pasta is cooking. After a few minutes remove a ladleful of pasta water and process with half the pecorino and the butter or olive oil to make a smooth sauce.

Drain the pasta, stir in the pecorino sauce and sprinkle over the remaining cheese. Grind a lot of black pepper over the pasta and serve at once.

Tagliatelle alla Panna
TAGLIATELLE WITH CREAM AND
CHEESE SAUCE

One of the fastest and most infamous of sauces. It was invented by the restaurant 'Alfredo' for Mary Pickford and Douglas Fairbanks, who rewarded Alfredo with a gold spoon and fork. Today it is almost forgotten as people have become more interested in healthy eating.

500g/1lb tagliatelle
50g/2oz butter
250ml/8fl oz double cream
200g/7oz freshly grated Parmesan
freshly ground black pepper

Melt half the butter in a pan and add the cream and half the cheese. Keep warm. Cook the pasta carefully to avoid over-cooking, drain and stir in the rest of the butter and cheese. When every strand is coated, stir in the cream sauce. Add freshly ground black pepper to taste and serve at once.

Spaghetti alla Gorgonzola
SPAGHETTI WITH GORGONZOLA
AND RICOTTA

500g/1lb spaghetti
90g/3½oz butter
1 stick celery, chopped
1 small onion, chopped
300ml/½ pint milk
150g/5oz Gorgonzola
300g/10oz ricotta
salt and black pepper

Heat the butter and add the chopped celery and onion. Cook gently without letting them turn colour. In a blender or food processor, purée the milk, Gorgonzola, ricotta and cooked vegetables. Turn into a saucepan and leave to heat through gently, stirring occasionally. Test for salt.

Cook the pasta, drain and stir in the butter and the warm cheese mixture. Turn into a heated serving dish, stir well and add black pepper to taste. Serve at once.

MEAT SAUCES

Bacon
Pancetta

The two following recipes are typically Roman and can be found all over the capital. Purists insist that *guanciale*, the tender succulent cut obtained from the pig's cheek, must be used for these sauces, but even in Rome bacon is used just as successfully.

Spaghetti alla Carbonara
CHARCOAL-MAKERS' SPAGHETTI

This very Roman pasta dish is thought to have been invented by the charcoal-burners who used to spend days in the hills outside Rome, turning the stacked wood piles into charcoal to be used for cooking before gas was piped through the city. It seems simple but in fact timing is very important to avoid producing pasta with scrambled eggs!

500g/1lb spaghetti
5 eggs
200ml/⅓ pint single cream or milk (optional,
not traditional)
2tbsp freshly grated Parmesan
1tbsp freshly grated pecorino
1tbsp extra virgin olive oil
150g/5oz guanciale or streaky bacon, diced
salt and freshly ground black pepper

Put a large saucepan of water on to boil.

Beat the eggs and add the cream, if using. Stir in the grated cheese and a little pepper.

In a large pan heat the oil and cook the guanciale on a low heat until the fat starts to run out. This will happen more quickly if you are substituting bacon. Remove from the heat.

Salt the boiling pasta water and throw in the spaghetti. When the pasta is still very al dente put the guanciale pan back on the heat, drain the pasta and stir into the guanciale. Remove the pan from the heat and, working quickly, stir in the egg mixture so that every strand of pasta is coated with a thick yellow cream. Take great care not to let the eggs coagulate. Serve at once with extra black pepper to hand.

Spaghetti alla Gricia and Bucatini all'Amatriciana
SPAGHETTI FROM GRICIANO AND AMATRICE

This rustic recipe comes from Griciano, in the Sabine hills, not far from the town of Amatrice. Romans took the dish and made it their own, as they did with the Sabine women in ancient times! When peeled, chopped tomato or tomato sauce is added with the garlic and onion the dish becomes pasta *all'Amatriciana*.

500g/1lb bucatini or spaghetti
3tbsp olive oil
1 small chilli pepper
200g/7oz guanciale or pancetta or streaky bacon
1 small onion, finely chopped
2 cloves garlic, finely chopped
100g/4oz freshly grated pecorino
2 red tomatoes, peeled and chopped (for Amatriciana)
salt

Gently heat 1 tablespoon of the olive oil, add the chilli to the pan, and the guanciale. Let the fat slowly melt into the oil, then remove the guanciale and add the finely chopped onion and garlic. Cook gently until golden brown, discard the chilli, and return the guanciale to the pan and keep warm.

Cook the pasta in briskly boiling salted water, drain, and toss in the pecorino before stirring in the onion and bacon mixture. To make the dish 'Amatriciana' add the chopped tomatoes at the end.

Ham

Proscuitto

In Italy the types of ham are legion. The most delicately flavoured cured ham – *proscuitto crudo* – comes from Parma or San
Daniele near Venice. Sliced wafer-thin by machine, the moist,
succulent ham, served with fresh figs or melon makes a delicious summer appetiser. This ham is known as dolce – sweet
– because it is not as salty as the proscuitto served with pickled
artichokes and olives, or the *prosciutto di montagna* (which has a
much stronger flavour and is usually sliced by hand).

Cooked ham, known as *proscuitto cotto*, is not part of the
Italian culinary tradition. However imported cooked ham has
become more widely used, not as an alternative to proscuitto
crudo but as an extra ingredient on a platter of hors d'oeuvre, or
antipasto.

Scrigno
JEWEL BOX PASTA

This recipe comes from a restaurant outside Rome, along the
old Appian Way. Just outside the Aurelian wall, amid the cata-
combs and reminders of early Christian Rome, is the crenel-
lated tower of the tomb of the Roman matron, Cecilia Metella.
She was the daughter-in-law of the wealthy Crassus, who first

financed the young Julius Caesar. Presumably she owes her ostentatiously large memorial to her rich in-laws.

Nearby is a trattoria that has a beautiful rose garden with tables around a fountain. Their speciality is served in individual bowls, shaped like the top of the Cecilia Metella tower. It is called scrigno, which means jewel box, suggesting all the delights concealed under the 'lid' of melted cheese.

500g/1lb fine green pasta or paglia e fieno
1 x quantity of tomato sauce (see page 90)
200ml/⅓ pint double cream
150g/5oz freshly grated Parmesan
6 thin slices ham
300g/10oz mozzarella
butter, for greasing

Preheat the oven to 220°C/425°F/gas 7.

Set aside 6 tablespoons of the tomato sauce. Stir the cream into the rest of the tomato sauce together with 1 tablespoonful of the grated Parmesan. Simmer for 10 minutes.

Cook the pasta for half the time given in the packet instructions. Drain and add to the tomato and cream sauce, stirring thoroughly.

Butter individual ovenproof bowls and fill two-thirds full with the pasta mixture. Cover each serving with a slice of ham cut into 6 pieces to make it easier to eat when cooked. Now cover this with thin slices of mozzarella. Put the reserved tomato sauce on top and then sprinkle with the remaining Parmesan. Cook in the oven for 20 minutes.

Paglia e Fieno alla Ciociara
PAGLIA E FIENO FARMHOUSE STYLE

A ciociara is the long wooden shoe originally worn by farm-workers outside Rome. The name has been given to a quick, easy sauce that is a favourite.

500g/1lb paglia e fieno or tagliatelle
150g/5oz shelled peas (fresh or frozen)
30g/1oz butter
150g/5oz white mushrooms, sliced
200g/7oz ham, chopped
250ml/8fl oz double cream
100g/4oz freshly grated Parmesan
salt and black pepper

If using fresh peas, cook in a little boiling water for 10 minutes; drain. Melt the butter and add the peas and sliced mushrooms. After 5 minutes, add the chopped ham and stir for a few minutes before adding the cream. Add salt and keep warm. Cook the pasta, drain and turn into a heated serving dish. Add the grated cheese and stir rapidly. Pour on the sauce, mix well, add freshly ground black pepper to taste and serve at once.

Meat
Carne

For someone not born in Naples it is difficult to appreciate what *ragù* signifies to a Neapolitan. At one time it was the traditional Sunday lunch for a large part of Naples and for many the one time in the week they could allow themselves the luxury of eating meat. The aroma of *ragù* used to drift along the narrow winding alleys and up over the roof tops until it seemed to many the perfume of Sunday. The *ragù* needs long, slow cooking and to avoid burning it needs to be watched as carefully as a new-born baby, as the Neapolitans say. Since this watching period lasts for three or four hours, it demands patience and a high degree of dedication. Gradually cooking *ragù* came to be seen as an expression of love, care and affection.

The great Neapolitan playwright, Eduardo de Filippo, shows this in a delightful little poem. The speaker criticises his wife's *ragù* saying that his mother made real *ragù* while his wife only produces meat and tomatoes. Clearly it is not only her cooking that is being held in question.

In Naples today, with all the pressures of modern life, the making of the real *ragù* is reserved for special occasions. Puppa Sicca learned to cook *ragù* as a present for her future husband before their formal engagement was announced. She usually makes it three or four times a year and I felt a great sense of warmth and affection when she prepared it for me one day. Here is her recipe. Readers familiar with Eduardo de Filippo's play, 'Saturday, Sunday, Monday', can compare notes.

Zitoni col Ragù Napoletano
ZITONI WITH NEAPOLITAN MEAT SAUCE

This is traditionally cooked in an earthenware pot but any large heavy pan may be used.

500g/1lb zitoni or spaghetti
700g/1½lb leg of pork
60g/2½oz butter
60g/2½oz margarine
6tbsp olive oil
1 onion, chopped
1 carrot, chopped
1 bay leaf
300g/10oz rib pork chops all in one piece
1 Neapolitan salami, skinned (if available)
a small glass of white wine
a small glass of red wine

1.5 litres/2½ pints hot water
400g/14oz tomato paste
salt and black pepper

Tie the pork leg very firmly to keep it in shape. Put the butter, margarine, oil, onion and carrot, bay leaf and meat (with the salami if used) into the pan and begin to cook very gently, covered. This initial cooking period takes about 2 hours. From time to time turn the pieces of meat to brown them on all sides. As the meat gradually browns the onion will disappear.

Now is the time to take the lid off and start adding liquid to make the sauce. As the meat begins to stick, add the white wine a few drops at a time, stirring well with a wooden spoon all along the bottom of the pan. Continue in this way until all the white wine has been used. Now start adding the red wine while scraping the juices from the bottom of the pan in exactly the same way. When the red wine has evaporated, gradually add the tomato paste, stirring it in thoroughly.

When the tomato has become very dark, a little tepid water is gradually added. This period of gradually adding water usually takes another 3 hours. The sauce is now very dark. At this stage it may be left to cook on its own. Add about 1.5 litres/2½ pints of hot water and cook very slowly in the covered pan for another 4 or 5 hours, stirring every half hour or so. This process is known onomatopoeically as *pippiare*. As the meat begins to come away from the bones, remove the pork chops from the pan; the larger piece of pork leg can be removed an hour or two later. Check for seasoning, add salt and black pepper.

The first part of this cooking is usually done the day before and the last few hours on the day itself, but there is no reason why it should not all be cooked in advance. Cook the pasta just before the meal, drain, turn into a serving bowl and stir in the meat sauce. The meat is served separately as a second course.

Fusilli con Polpettine
FUSILLI WITH MEATBALLS

Several times I have heard experts on Italian cooking state categorically that spaghetti and meatballs is an American innovation unknown in Italy. This is not true, however.

It is important to remember that Italy is divided by its geography, history and culture and only became unified, politically speaking, in the last century. Culinary traditions are still very regional. A Florentine may never have eaten pasta with meatballs, but it is common in the south, which was the birthplace of many Italian Americans. In Puglia, meatballs are cooked in a tomato sauce and either eaten with the pasta or served separately afterwards.

The traditional Carnevale Lasagne from Naples always contains meatballs, and they are found in several other recipes in Southern Italy.

500g/1lb fusilli or other short pasta
2 cloves garlic
400g/14oz lean boneless veal, beef or pork
2 small slices white bread, crusts removed
1tbsp chopped parsley
100g/4oz freshly grated Parmesan
2 eggs
4tbsp olive oil
1 onion, finely chopped

a small glass of white wine
400g/14oz tin Italian plum tomatoes, sieved or processed
a little stock
salt and black pepper
flour, for dusting

Work the garlic and meat in a food processor or through a mincer, then add the bread, chopped parsley and half the grated cheese. Mix thoroughly with the eggs and season to taste. Roll into small balls about the size of a walnut and flour lightly.

Heat the oil, add the onion and cook until it has softened but not turned colour. Add the meatballs and cook over a low heat until lightly browned on all sides. Now add the wine and boil to reduce to half the quantity. Add the tomatoes and a very little stock. Cover and cook for about 1 hour.

Cook the pasta, drain and turn into a warmed serving bowl. Stir in the sauce, meatballs and the rest of the cheese and serve.

Tagliatelle alla Bolognese
TAGLIATELLE WITH BOLOGNESE SAUCE

Bolognese must be the most well-known of all Italian pasta sauces and is certainly the most falsified. Counterfeit Bolognese sauce appears on menus all over the world and should usually be avoided. I am tempted to say only eat Bolognese sauce if you are in or around Bologna, or if you have made it yourself. Any sauce using minced meat does not automatically qualify to be called Bolognese, and most of the poor imitations around bear no resemblance to the rich, opulent sauce which is the triumph of the glorious Emilian cooking tradition.

500g/1lb tagliatelle or egg pasta
1tbsp tomato paste
150ml/4fl oz hot stock
2tbsp olive oil
80g/3oz butter
1 medium onion, minced
1 carrot, minced
1 celery stalk, minced
100g/4oz bacon, finely chopped
150g/5oz lean boneless pork, minced
150g/5oz lean boneless beef, minced
50g/2oz fresh Italian sausage or pure sausage meat,
skin removed
a small glass of white wine
75ml/3fl oz double cream
freshly grated Parmesan, to serve (optional)
salt and black pepper

Dilute the tomato paste in the stock. Heat the oil and 50g/2oz of the butter and add the minced onion, carrot and celery and finely chopped bacon. Cook gently for about 10 minutes, then add the pork and beef, sausage meat and wine. Cook gently for a further 10 minutes, stirring from time to time. Now add the tomato stock mixture. Stir and add seasoning to taste. Cook gently for 1½ hours.

Stir in the cream and when it has been absorbed by the sauce remove from the heat and keep warm. Cook the pasta carefully to avoid overcooking. Meanwhile, return the sauce to the heat and stir in the remaining butter. Drain the pasta, turn into a heated serving dish and add the sauce.

Note: This dish is often served without stirring in the sauce: the sauce sits in the middle of the circle of drained pasta. It is probably best to bring the dish to the table in its glory, but stir well before serving. Serve freshly grated cheese separately if desired.

Rigatoni alla Genovese
RIGATONI WITH GENOVESE SAUCE

This is one of the main Neapolitan sauces and plays an important role in the history of the cooking of Naples, yet it is something of a culinary mystery. The name means 'in the style of Genoa' but the sauce itself is unknown in Genoa. The use of onions in this quantity seems to suggest a French influence and the finished dish has certain affinities with Boeuf à la Mode. The most likely explanation seems to be that the sauce was introduced to Naples by one of the many Genovese merchants who settled there in the 15th century.

Although this dish is quite time-consuming to prepare, like several other recipes from the south of Italy, it supplies both first and second course. The sauce is used with pasta and the meat is then sliced and served with different vegetables afterwards.

500g/1lb rigatoni or any other short pasta
6tbsp olive oil
100g/4oz raw ham with rind, finely chopped
1 small carrot, finely chopped
1 stick celery, finely chopped
1kg/2lb lean cut of beef such as topside, tied
with string to keep its shape
2kg/4lb onions, thinly sliced

a small glass of white wine
150ml/¼ pint hot stock
100g/4oz freshly grated Parmesan
salt and black pepper

Heat the oil in a narrow saucepan just big enough to take the meat and vegetables. When the oil is hot add the ham and chopped vegetables and stir well over a low heat for 5 minutes. Now add the meat and onions. The meat should be completely covered by the onions. Add 50ml/2fl oz water and salt and pepper to taste.

Cover and cook over a moderate heat, stirring from time to time, until the onions and meat begin to turn golden brown. Now turn the heat to very low and begin the slow-cooking process. This involves the same techniques as with the Neapolitan *ragù* (see page 132), known as *tirata*, as the flavour is 'pulled' out of the meat into the sauce. A little of the wine and then stock needs to be added each time the sauce is stirred if it appears to be sticking to the bottom of the pan. Stir vigorously under the meat with a wooden spoon at very short intervals because the addition of too much liquid ruins the sauce. A Neapolitan cook will spend about 2 hours minimum over this part of the recipe. When the cooking process is finished the sauce will be almost chestnut-coloured and the long cooking makes use of a blender or processor unnecessary. The sauce can be prepared the day before if required. The meat is usually allowed to cool before slicing.

Cook the pasta, drain, reserving a little of the pasta water to add to the sauce before stirring it into the pasta. The Parmesan is stirred into the pasta before the sauce is added or it can be served separately at table.

Malloreddus con il Ragù di Agnello alla Sarda
SARDINIAN PASTA WITH LAMB SAUCE

The life in the interior of Sardinia bears no resemblance to the convivial *dolce vita* of the Costa Smeralda. The land is austere and largely uninhabited. The shepherds lead a nomadic life for long periods of the year to graze their sheep on the poor pasture. Sardinian cooking is based on the rhythms of this life.

Meat is usually roasted in the open air over a spit and the sweet-smelling juniper and olive wood add a particular flavour to the meat. No eggs are used in the traditional pasta, which is made from flour, water, salt and a pinch of saffron. This pasta is rolled into a small oval form called *malloreddus* which means baby calf. A fresh cheese is made from the ewes' milk and the matured Sardinian pecorino (pecorino *sardo*) is known and appreciated far and wide.

500g/1lb malloreddus or other short pasta
1 small leg of lamb (approx. 1kg/2lb)
2 cloves garlic, finely sliced
6tbsp olive oil
a few sprigs of rosemary
1 small onion, finely sliced
400g/14oz tin Italian plum tomatoes, chopped
salt and black pepper
50g/2oz freshly grated pecorino sardo or romano
cheese, to serve

Preheat the oven to 325°F/170°C/gas 3.

With a sharp, pointed knife, make several small incisions all along the leg of lamb and insert slivers of garlic and sprigs of rosemary. Rub the leg with salt, pepper and some of the oil. Heat the rest of the oil in a pan that can be transferred to the oven later. Brown the lamb all over, then add the finely sliced onion and the chopped tomatoes with their juice. Add more salt and pepper if necessary. Cover with foil and cook slowly in the oven for 2 hours, adding a little water if the sauce becomes too dry. When the meat is cooked, the sauce is used with the pasta and the meat is served as the second course.

Cook the pasta, following the packet directions carefully to avoid overcooking. Drain the pasta, reserving 60ml/2½fl oz of the pasta water to add to the sauce. Turn the pasta into a heated serving bowl and stir in the sauce. Grated cheese should be served separately.

Pappardelle con la Lepre
WIDE RIBBON PASTA WITH HARE SAUCE

500g/1lb pappardelle or tagliatelle
2tbsp olive oil
50g/2oz butter
50g/2oz bacon, finely chopped
1 small onion, finely chopped
1 stick celery, finely chopped
600g/1¼lb meat cut from a hare, cut
into very small cubes
1tbsp chopped thyme
1tbsp flour
a small glass of white wine
500ml/16fl oz boiling concentrated stock
salt and black pepper
freshly grated Parmesan, to serve

Heat the oil and butter in a pan and gently fry the bacon, onion and celery. Add the meat and season with salt, pepper and thyme. When the meat is browned, sprinkle with the flour; stir and brown the flour. Add the wine and when that has almost evaporated add the boiling stock. Cover and cook gently for 2 hours.

Cook the pasta, drain and turn into a heated serving bowl. Stir in the sauce. Grated Parmesan should be served separately.

Spaghetti alla Chitarra col Ragù di Maiale
SPAGHETTI ALLA CHITARRA WITH PORK SAUCE

The Abruzzi is a region of great contrasts stretching from the Adriatic Sea at Pescara to the ski resorts in the Appennines. The cooking of the Abruzzi has long been prized by the rest of Italy. The local pasta speciality is spaghetti *alla chitarra*. The fresh pasta is made with eggs and rolled out less thinly than for tagliatelle. A traditional instrument made of wood with steel wires stretching from end to end – hence the name *chitarra* or guitar – is used to cut the pasta into long strands. The sheet of pasta is placed on the wires and the rolling pin is rolled up and down over the sheet until the pasta falls in thick, uniform lengths between the wires. If it is not available fine tagliatelle may be used.

500g/1lb spaghetti alla chitarra or tagliatelle
60g/2½oz lard
1 large onion, finely chopped
1 small chilli pepper
120g/4½oz minced pork
230g/8oz tin Italian plum
tomatoes, chopped

salt
100g/4oz freshly grated pecorino or
Parmesan, to serve

Melt the lard in a pan and add the onion and the chilli pepper.
After 5 minutes, add the pork and stir around until it begins to
brown. Now add the tomatoes with their juice and salt to taste
and cook for about 30 minutes. Remove the chilli. Cook the
pasta, drain, then turn into a heated serving bowl and stir in the
sauce. The grated cheese should be served separately.

Spaghetti con Sugo della Piazzaiola
SPAGHETTI WITH PIZZAIOLA SAUCE

Another recipe from the south, in which the sauce is used for
pasta and the meat is then served separately with vegetables.

500g/1lb spaghetti
3½tbsp olive oil
6 thin slices veal or beef
1tbsp chopped parsley
2 cloves garlic, chopped
½tsp capers
400g/14oz tin Italian plum tomatoes
salt
freshly grated Parmesan, to serve (optional)

Put the olive oil and 125ml/4½fl oz water in a pan and heat
together. (This is done because the meat must stew, not fry.)
Add the meat with a little chopped parsley, the chopped garlic,

capers and tomatoes with their juice. Add salt to taste. Cook gently for 35 minutes. Cook the pasta, drain and stir in the sauce. Parmesan is usually served separately.

Sausages
Salsiccie

Norcia in Umbria is the home of such excellent pork products that in central Italy a shop specialising in sausages and hams is called a *norceria* and a pasta sauce made from fresh sausages is called *norcina*. Italian sausages are made solely from meat and since they contain quite a lot of fat they are pricked before being cooked slowly in white wine, to enable the fat to run out. For these recipes use good quality meat sausages without additional bread or soya filler.

Rigatoni alla Norcina
RIGATONI WITH NORCIA SAUCE

500g/1lb rigatoni or short pasta
1tbsp olive oil
1 small onion, finely sliced
200g/7oz pork sausages
100ml/3½fl oz white wine
250ml/8fl oz double cream
50g/2oz freshly grated Parmesan
salt and black pepper

Heat the oil and fry the onion slowly in a covered pan. The onion should not be allowed to change colour. Remove the skin from the sausages and divide the meat into very small pieces. Put them in the pan with the onion and add the wine. After 10 minutes, add the cream and simmer gently, uncovered, for about 10 minutes. Remove from heat, add salt to taste, and keep warm.

Cook the pasta, drain, toss in the grated cheese and turn into a heated serving dish. Stir in the sauce, add freshly ground black pepper to taste and serve at once.

Conchiglie alla Burina
SHELLS WITH RUSTIC SAUCE

The countryman who sold his butter, or *burro*, in Roman markets was called a *burino*, but in modern Rome the term merely means bad-mannered. This sauce takes its name from the original meaning.

500g/1lb conchiglie or other short pasta
40g/1½oz butter
1 small onion, finely chopped
1 clove garlic, finely chopped
400g/14oz tin Italian plum tomatoes
200g/7oz large pork sausages
a small glass of white wine
150g/5oz shelled peas
salt and black pepper

Melt the butter and add the finely chopped onion and garlic. When the onion begins to turn colour add the tomatoes with their juice. Season to taste with salt and black pepper. Cook for 20 minutes.

Meanwhile, prick the sausages and cook them gently in the wine in a separate, covered pan. When they are cooked, strain their liquid into the tomatoes. Skin the sausages and slice them into rounds.

Cook the pasta, following the packet directions carefully to avoid overcooking. Add the peas to the tomato sauce and cook until just tender. Before draining the pasta, add the sausage to the sauce. Drain the pasta, turn into a warm serving dish and stir in the sauce. Serve at once.

STRAVAGANZE –
SPECIAL OCCASION
PASTA

Crêpes
Crespelle

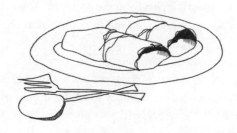

Crêpes with a fine pasta stuffing make a sumptuous first course for a dinner party. Use tagliolini and choose one of the creamy, delicate sauces. I like to make green crêpes with spinach and basil – spinach for the colour, basil for the flavour – filled with tagliolini in a smoked salmon sauce.

Crespelle Alexander
CRÊPES ALEXANDER

250g/9oz tagliolini (tagliarini)
250ml/8fl oz milk
2 eggs
120g/4½oz flour
100g/4oz spinach, boiled and squeezed dry

8 basil leaves (optional)
1 x quantity Tagliolini al Salmone sauce (see page 167)
a small jar of coral salmon eggs (optional)
butter, for frying

Preheat the oven to 180°C/350°F/gas 4.

Blend the milk, eggs, flour, spinach and basil leaves (if using) in a food processor or blender. When the batter is smooth, fry in butter in a non-stick pan to make 6 crêpes. The crêpes should be cooked in advance and allowed to cool so that they are easier to handle.

Use the Tagliolini al Salmone for the pasta filling. The cream-coloured tagliolini make a contrast with the green crêpe and coral-coloured sauce. The secret is to make the smoked salmon sauce in exactly the same quantity as given in the recipe on page 167, but to cook only half the amount of pasta. The extra sauce is used to pour over the crêpes.

Cook the pasta and stir in half the sauce. Put one sixth of the pasta in the middle of a crêpe, roll it up and place it, seam down, in a buttered oven dish long enough to take the six crêpes in one layer. When all 6 crêpes are stuffed, pour the rest of the sauce over the top and bake for 15 minutes. If I am feeling extravagant I buy a small jar of coral salmon eggs and trail them over the top just before serving.

Moulded pasta

In Naples and the south of Italy there is a strong tradition of ornamental dishes made up of various meat fillings cooked in a pasta mould and then turned out to present a spectacular first course.

Bucatini alla Flamande is an ancient recipe now almost forgotten. No one knows the origin of its name but the recipe itself must date back to the time when the *monzù* – as Neapolitans called their French chefs – were creating masterpieces for the great aristocratic houses.

Prince Francesco d'Avalos first told me of the existence of this recipe and I am grateful to have learned its secrets from him. The prince's family came to Naples from Spain in the 15th century with Alfonso of Aragon and today, in the beautiful Palazzo d'Avalos in Naples, he and his chef Herman Piacenti, who prepared this dish for me, still keep the great Neapolitan culinary tradition alive for their appreciative friends.

Tinned copper moulds have been specially made for the Palazzo d'Avalos kitchens by local craftsmen, but the dish can be prepared successfully in a heat-resistant ice cream bombe mould or an ordinary 1.2 litre/2 pintlidded pudding basin.

I tried this recipe substituting mushrooms for black truffles and found the filling a little anaemic, but the same technique of lining a mould with bucatini can be used to advantage with shellfish or any other special filling when black truffles are not available.

Bucatini alla Flamande
BUCATINI IN A MOULD

250g/9oz bucatini (no other pasta will do)
200g/7oz lean boneless meat
1 carrot
1 onion
1 stick celery
1tbsp chopped parsley
2 egg whites
500ml/16fl oz béchamel sauce (see page 80)
50g/2oz cooked tongue, cubed
150g/5oz cooked chicken breast meat, flaked
150g/5oz cooked ham, cubed
15g/½ oz black truffles, chopped
salt and black pepper
butter, for greasing

for the sauce:
200g/7oz meat in one piece
1tbsp olive oil
2 carrots, chopped
1 onion, chopped
2 sticks celery, chopped
1 clove garlic, chopped
250ml/8fl oz hot stock
salt and black pepper

In a food processor, turn the raw meat, carrot, onion, celery, parsley and egg whites into a fine paste. Season to taste. Add about one-third of the béchamel sauce to the paste in the processor. Keep the paste thick.

To make the sauce, brown the piece of meat in the oil and then add the chopped vegetables. Stir until they are well browned, then add a little stock and cook gently for about 1 hour. Remove the meat and purée the vegetables to make a smooth sauce. Add more stock if necessary. Season to taste and set aside.

Cook the bucatini for half the time stated in the packet instructions; drain. Butter the mould. Take a single strand of bucatini and begin to roll it into a coil in your hand. Place it in the bottom of the mould and gradually coil in more strands of bucatini, sticking them against the buttered sides of the mould to form a lining of coiled bucatini. This is a very slow and fiddly process but the finished effect is worth the effort. Do not worry about the joins in the bucatini; they even out in cooking.

When all the mould has been lined, use a palette knife to plaster the meat and béchamel paste over the bucatini lining, as a bricklayer uses cement. When all the bucatini lining has been pasted firmly to the sides of the mould, begin to fill the mould with a little of the tongue, chicken, ham and truffles, then a spoonful of béchamel sauce and a few strands of bucatini.

Continue this filling process in layers until the mould is full. Finish with a coiled lid of bucatini covered with a generous layer of paste. Cover with buttered paper and then the lid, tied firmly in place.

Cook in a bain-marie of warm water on top of the stove for 45 minutes. At the end of this time, remove the lid and paper and turn out on to a warmed serving plate.

The pasta mould will look like an exotic beehive. I prefer to serve the reheated sauce separately to avoid masking the beautiful appearance of the unmoulded pasta.

How to line the mould

1) Place a coil of pasta in the base of the mould and coil around the sides.

2) Plaster the sides of the bucatini mould with the meat paste then fill with the meat, truffle and sauce.

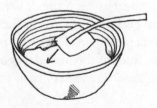

3) Finish the 'lid' with a coil of pasta and a layer of meat paste.

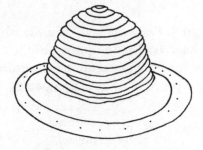

Pasta Cooked in Foil Parcels

Spaghetti al Cartoccio
SPAGHETTI WITH SHELLFISH IN FOIL

This recipe, from 'Il Pescatore', can be made with any mixture of shellfish, so you can adapt the quantities if you do not find all the ingredients. The silver parcel looks spectacular when carried to the table and opened in front of your guests.

500g/1lb spaghetti
500g/1lb mussels
500g/1lb small clams
100g/4oz tiny squid
3½tbsp olive oil
2 cloves garlic, chopped
1 small chilli pepper, chopped, or 1tsp dried chilli flakes
150g/5oz unshelled raw prawns or shrimps
400g/14oz tin Italian plum tomatoes
a small glass of white wine
1tbsp chopped parsley
salt

Preheat the oven to 220°C/425°F/gas 7.

Scrub the mussels and clams well with a stiff brush or pot scourer. Discard any mussel or clam that is open or has a broken shell. Put them in a little water over a low heat and cook just until their shells open. This will make sure that any sand comes out and does not go into your pasta sauce.

Very small squid are usually served whole. If using larger squid, cut the sack into rings, remove and discard the head and the hard part in the middle of the ring joining the tentacles, and cut the rest into small pieces.

Heat the oil in a large pan and add the chopped garlic and the chilli pepper. When the garlic begins to turn colour, add the small squid and the prawns. After 5 minutes add the mussels and clams, tomatoes and wine. Season with salt and cook for 10 minutes.

The spaghetti should be cooked for only half the time stated in the packet instructions. Drain the pasta and very quickly, mix it with the hot shellfish sauce and chopped parsley. Have a double layer of foil ready on a baking sheet. Put the spaghetti mixture in the middle and fold over the foil, making sure all the folds are tightly closed to prevent any steam escaping. Cook in the oven for 8 minutes.

Carry the foil parcel to the table. Open, stir well with a wooden fork and serve from the foil. The aroma that comes out in the cloud of steam has to be experienced to be believed.

Note: The shellfish are served in their shells so put small plates on the table for the shells to be discarded as the shellfish are eaten.

Pastry Cases
Timballi

For important occasions pasta is traditionally served inside a pastry case. Giuseppe di Lampedusa in *The Leopard* describes how the Prince delighted his guests by serving macaroni pie at the solemn dinner held on the first night of his visit to his country estate, Donnafugata, in Sicily:

> Three lackeys in green, gold and powder entered, each holding a great silver dish containing a towering macaroni pie.

The pie crust was always made from sweet pastry in contrast to the savoury filling inside:

> Good manners apart, though, the aspect of those monumental dishes of macaroni was worthy of the quivers of admiration they evoked. The burnished gold of the crusts, the fragrance of sugar and cinnamon they exuded, were but preludes to the delights released from the interior when the knife broke the crust; first came a spice-laden haze, then chicken livers, hard-boiled eggs,

sliced ham, chicken and truffles in masses of piping hot, glistening macaroni, to which the meat juice gave an exquisite hue of suede.

Timballo del Gattopardo
TIMBALLO FROM THE LEOPARD

for the pastry:
500g/1lb flour
a pinch of salt
1tsp ground cinnamon
150g/5oz sugar
150g/5oz butter
water, to mix

for the filling:
500g/1lb short pasta
1 chicken (1.5kg/3lb)
500g/1lb piece of beef (optional)
1 stick celery
1 onion or 2 carrots
5 eggs
100g/4oz freshly grated Parmesan
a large bunch of fresh parsley, chopped
4tbsp olive oil
120g/4½oz chicken livers
150g/5oz shelled peas
100g/4oz cooked ham, cut into strips
1 small black truffle, sliced (optional)
salt and black pepper
butter, for greasing

Make the pastry and chill for at least 1 hour. I prefer to avoid the sweet/savoury combination so I omit the sugar and cinnamon.

Preheat the oven to 180°C/350°F/gas 4.

Boil the chicken with the small piece of beef, if using, the celery and onion and or carrots. Drain the chicken and strain the stock.

Take 200g/7oz of the cooked chicken meat and either mince or process it with 1 egg, two-thirds of the Parmesan, parsley, and salt and pepper to taste. When you have a soft, paste-like consistency, roll it into balls the size of cherries. Fry the balls in the olive oil; they should barely change colour.

Cut the rest of the chicken meat into strips. Simmer the chicken livers for a few moments in a little water with salt and pepper. When cooked, cut into small pieces. Cook the peas. Hard-boil the remaining eggs. All the above preparation can be done well in advance.

Roll out two-thirds of the pastry to make a circle large enough to line a deep, well-buttered oven dish. Roll out the rest of the pastry to make a lid for the pie. Heat 400ml/14fl oz of the strained stock and add the chicken, ham, chicken livers, meat-balls and peas. Remove from the heat. Add the sliced truffle if available. Cook the pasta for half the time stated in the packet instructions; drain. Add half the pasta to the meat mixture and put the other half into the pastry case, arranging it around the outer edges and leaving a space in the middle. Put the pasta and sauce into the middle space and spoon over the top of the plain pasta. Arrange the hard-boiled eggs, each cut into 8 segments, over the top and cover with the rest of the grated cheese.

Cover with the other piece of pastry and seal the edges well with a little milk. Bake in the oven for about 40 minutes.

Timballo per la Domenica delle Palme
MACARONI PIE FOR PALM SUNDAY

This is made with fish and is served on Palm Sunday in Naples. Although this recipe traditionally uses a sweet pastry casing, I am giving a version which I think is more acceptable to modern tastes.

for the pastry:
500g/1lb flour
a pinch of salt
250g/9oz butter
2 eggs
water, to mix

for the filling:
500g/1lb spaghetti or vermicelli
500g/1lb filleted white fish such as cod
100g/4oz pitted black olives
3tbsp drained capers
30g/1oz pine nuts, shelled walnuts or blanched almonds
a large bunch of fresh parsley, chopped
250ml/8fl oz olive oil
4tbsp fresh breadcrumbs
100g/4oz shelled peas
500ml/16fl oz tomato sauce (see recipe page 90)
100g/4oz mushrooms, sliced
500g/1lb shellfish such as mussels, clams, etc.
1tbsp cornflour, dissolved in a little water
2 cloves garlic, chopped
6 anchovy fillets, finely chopped

salt and black pepper
butter, for greasing

Preheat the oven to 180°C/350°F/gas 4. Make the pastry and chill for at least 1 hour.

Butter a large, round ovenproof dish. Roll out two-thirds of the pastry and use to line the dish. Roll out the rest of the pastry to make a large lid for the pie, then put it on a greased baking tray and bake both blind for 10 minutes in the oven and allow to cool.

In a food processor, process the raw white fish, pitted olives, capers, nuts, some of the parsley, and salt and pepper to taste. Add 2 tablespoons of the oil and 2 tablespoons of breadcrumbs. If the mixture seems too wet, add more breadcrumbs. Roll this mixture into balls the size of walnuts. Coat the balls lightly in breadcrumbs and fry in a little olive oil until they begin to turn colour. Add the fish balls and shelled peas to the tomato sauce. Leave to cook gently.

Cook the mushrooms lightly in a little oil, then add them to the tomato sauce.

Cook the shellfish in a little water until they have opened. Remove them from their shells and add to the sauce. Strain the cooking liquid and add to the sauce as well. Stir the cornflour into the sauce to thicken it.

Heat 3½ tablespoons of olive oil in a separate pan and add the chopped garlic. When the garlic turns colour, discard it and add the anchovies and some chopped parsley to the oil.

Cook the pasta for half the time given in the packet instructions. Drain and stir in the anchovy sauce.

Put a layer of pasta in the pastry case, followed by a layer of tomato sauce. Then add another layer of pasta and another layer of tomato sauce. Finish with a layer of pasta.

Put the pastry lid on top and cook in the oven for 40 minutes.

Pasta in Pastry

It is possible to serve any of the more delicate pasta recipes inside a large vol-au-vent casing. A vol-au-vent filled with small tortellini in the cream, pea and ham sauce on page 130 makes an elegant first course.

I also like to make a quiche-style pastry case and fill it with small pasta shells or quills and the courgette sauce on page 49. For an elegant topping, I arrange thin overlapping slices of courgettes which have been cooked for 5 minutes in boiling salted water, over the top of the pasta, covered by a light sprinkling of Parmesan and black pepper, and baked for 15 minutes in a moderate oven, 180°C/350°F/gas 4.

Soufflé
Soufflé

One of the many ways to dress up pasta for a party is to make it the foundation for a soufflé. It was one of the favourite dishes of the late composer Sir William Walton, and was prepared for him in his house on the island of Ischia by his cook, Reale.

Zitoni all'Impiedi
SOUFFLE WITH STANDING-UP PASTA

400g/14oz zitoni or wide tube pasta
50g/2oz butter
40g/1½oz Parmesan
100g/4oz cooked ham, cut into 8cm/3¼ inch sticks
150g/5oz mozzarella, cut into 8cm/3¼ inch sticks
butter, for greasing

for the soufflé mixture:
80g/3oz butter
60g/2½oz flour
300ml/½ pint milk
6 eggs, separated
80g/3oz freshly grated Parmesan
80g/3oz freshly grated emmenthal
1tbsp chopped parsley
salt and black pepper

Preheat the oven to 150°C/300°F/gas 2. Butter a soufflé dish which is 25cm/10 inches in diameter and 10cm/4 inches high. Cook the zitoni whole for a mere 3 minutes. Drain but keep all the water. Cut the pasta into 8cm/3¼ inch lengths so that when stood up in the soufflé dish they come about 2cm/¾ inch below the top. Now reheat the pasta in its original water (bring to the boil again before adding the pasta), cook for 3 minutes and drain again. Stir in the butter and Parmesan.

Now comes the time-consuming process: stand a line of pasta tubes all around the inside edge of the dish. Inside the pasta make a border of alternating ham and mozzarella sticks. Now make another circle of pasta tubes, and continue like this until there is a space in the middle of about 7 to 8cm/3 to 3¼ inches in diameter. Discard any leftover pasta.

Make a béchamel sauce with the butter, flour and milk, and when it has cooled add the beaten egg yolks, the grated cheeses, chopped parsley and salt and pepper to taste. Beat the egg whites until they are stiff, then fold them gently into the cheese mixture. Spoon this mixture into the rings of pasta, making sure that all the tubes of pasta become filled. When all the tubes are full, put the remaining soufflé mixture into the empty space in the middle. Bake in the oven for 1 hour; do not open the oven door during this time. Serve immediately.

Caviar
Caviale

Spaghetti al Caviale
SPAGHETTI WITH CAVIAR SAUCE

500g/1lb spaghetti
60g/2½oz butter
200ml/⅓ pint double cream
60g/2½oz caviar
50g/2oz smoked salmon, cut into thin strips (optional)
freshly ground black pepper

Melt the butter over a low heat, stir in the cream and add freshly ground black pepper to taste. Simmer for 2 minutes and put aside.

Put the pasta on to cook. Meanwhile, return the cream to the heat and stir in the caviar and smoked salmon, if using. Drain the pasta, stir in the sauce, turn on to a heated serving dish and serve at once.

Smoked Salmon
Salmone Affumicato

Tagliolini al Salmone
TAGLIOLINI WITH SMOKED SALMON

A luxury sauce prepared in five minutes flat.

500g/1lb tagliolini (tagliarini)
30g/1oz butter
½ small onion, finely chopped
150g/5oz smoked salmon
200ml/⅓ pint single cream
freshly ground black pepper

Melt the butter and cook the onion until it is soft but has not changed colour. Add half the smoked salmon, roughly chopped, and the cream. Warm gently, then blend or process together with the onion until smooth. Cut the rest of the salmon into thin strips, using kitchen scissors.

Cook the pasta, drain and turn into a serving bowl. Add the cream and salmon sauce. Stir thoroughly and add a little freshly ground black pepper. Gently stir in the salmon strips and serve at once.

Truffles
Tartufi

A few shavings of fresh truffle turn a simple dish into an opulent, exotic feast. The truffle is particularly suited to dishes of egg, cheese or pasta, which act as a neutral foil to set off the heady flavour. White truffles should never be cooked, and black truffles are at their best when merely warmed gently.

The so-called white truffle looks like a clod of earth before it has been cleaned. It should be put in warm water to remove the mud, and any obstinate specks can be removed with a soft brush. Inside it is a delicate camel colour with traceries of fine white veins. Once the outside crust is off, however, it is difficult to notice the appearance. The alluring scent that comes from a truffle in season is an invitation to all the other senses.

White truffles are found mainly around Alba in Piedmont but some are discovered in Umbria near Norcia and Spoleto, the home of the black truffle. The white truffle is in season from October to December, followed by the black truffle in season from Christmas Eve until the end of March. Out of season, truffles have little perfume and are not worth eating, and unfortunately preserved truffles give little idea of the splendour of the fresh truffle.

In the mediaeval city of Spoleto, the Di Marco family's restaurant 'Il Tartufo' specialises in truffle dishes. They serve pasta covered with fragrant wafers of large, superbly-flavoured truffles which they buy directly from the local specialists.

Tagliatelle col Tartufo
TAGLIATELLE WITH TRUFFLE

500g/1lb tagliatelle
100g/4oz butter
100g/4oz freshly grated Parmesan
½ a small glass of white wine
1 small truffle
salt and black pepper

Heat 80g/3oz of the butter then stir in the cheese. When this has melted, add the white wine, and salt and pepper to taste. Cook the pasta, drain and turn into a heated serving dish. Stir in the remaining butter then the sauce. Cover the top with thin shavings of truffle. (In Italy there is a special tool for cutting truffles, but a very sharp paring knife can be used successfully.) Serve immediately.

Acknowledgements

When I wrote the original book in 1988 the following people helped enormously. Some of them are no longer with us but I would like to repeat my original Acknowledgments.

For many years I have been eating, cooking and talking about pasta with Italian friends. But I would particularly like to thank the following individuals for their help to me during that period that I was writing this book: in Naples, Francesco d'Avalos, Annamaria Visocchi Giovagnoli, Nello Oliviero and Pupa Sicca; in Ischia, Lady Walton; in Lecce, Sandra Della Notte and Emma Guagnano; and in Rome Rita Soccorsi, Ines Zerbini and Angelina di Mambro. Among those who gave me recipes from pasta dishes served in their restaurants, I would like to thank Guiseppe Palladino from 'Vecchia Roma', Filippo Porcelli from 'Checco er Carettiere', and Mario from 'Taverna Guilia', all in Rome. Also Salvatore Mellino from the trattoria, 'Maria Grazia', in Marina di Cantone, Emilio di Marco of 'Il Tartufo' in Spoleto, and Alberto and Domenico Zafrani from 'Il Pescatore' in Fiumicino. My special thanks to Robert Budwig, whose illustrations have so marvellously caught the spirit of Italy and its pasta dishes and to my editor, Maureen Green, for her skill and unfailing encouragement and support.

Diane Seed, 1988

Index